# The
# Amish Cook's Baking Book

# The Amish Cook's Baking Book

Lovina Eicher with Kevin Williams

Photography by Betsy Dellaposta

Andrews McMeel
Publishing, LLC
Kansas City · Sydney · London

To my husband and children

—Lovina

Also by Lovina Eicher with Kevin Williams
*The Amish Cook at Home: Simple Pleasures of Food, Family, and Faith*

*The Amish Cook's Baking Book* copyright © 2009 Lovina Eicher with Kevin Williams.
Photography © 2009 Betsy Dellaposta. All rights reserved. Printed in China. No part of
this book may be used or reproduced in any manner whatsoever without written permission
except in the case of reprints in the context of reviews. For information, write Andrews
McMeel Publishing, LLC, an Andrews McMeel Universal company, 1130 Walnut Street,
Kansas City, Missouri 64106.

09 10 11 12 13 POA 10 9 8 7 6 5 4 3 2 1

Library of Congress Cataloging-in-Publication Data

Eicher, Lovina.
  The Amish cook's baking book / Lovina Eicher with Kevin Williams ;
photography by Betsy Dellaposta.—1st ed.
    p. cm.
  ISBN-13: 978-0-7407-8547-4
  ISBN-10: 0-7407-8547-8
  1.  Baking. 2.  Amish cookery. 3.  Amish—Social life and customs.  I. Williams, Kevin. II.
Title.
  TX763.E53 2009
  641.5'66—dc22

                                                                    2009008907

Photos on pages 67, 90, 145 copyright © 2009 istockphoto.com

Design by Julie Barnes

www.andrewsmcmeel.com
www.amishcookonline.com

## ATTENTION: SCHOOLS AND BUSINESSES

Andrews McMeel books are available at quantity discounts with bulk purchase for educational,
business, or sales promotional use. For information, please write to: Special Sales Department,
Andrews McMeel Publishing, LLC, 1130 Walnut Street, Kansas City, Missouri 64106.

# CONTENTS

# Acknowledgments

*I would like to thank our editors at Andrews McMeel for their help with this endeavor. Also a special thanks to my husband, Joe, and my children, Elizabeth, Susan, Verena, Benjamin, Loretta, Joseph, Lovina, and Kevin. Making a book like this possible took a lot of consideration on my family's part. I appreciate all their willing help and support. Thanks also goes to my sister, Emma Schwartz, for her help and encouragement.*

*—Lovina Eicher*

I would like to thank the many behind-the-scenes hands who helped make this book possible. First of all, a big thank-you to my literary agent, Janis Donnaud. Janis is a living "road map" helping me navigate the book business. I'd also like to thank my editors at Andrews McMeel Publishing, Jean Lucas and Kirsty Melville, for their enthusiasm and willingness to work with us. Working with the Amish Cook requires a special degree of patience, without having e-mail or phone—essential tools of the trade—to work with. Special appreciation also to the AMP design team for their dynamite work and Tammie Barker for her help on promotions. Thanks also goes to Sharon Fuge, Shirley Diver, Jessica Alcorn, Ashleigh Diver, Dan Burleson, Randi Maerz, Paula Rees, Rebecca Shields, Mary Etta, Trish Hill, Alissa McKinney, Shelley Valdivia, Pam Rehder, Andrea Snyder, Barbara Wesley, Cathy Bailey, and Susie Conrad. Also, thank you to my wife, Rachel, for her patience and to Betsy Dellaposta for her great, respectful photography.

—Kevin Williams

# Introduction

*"When I was a young girl at home with my parents, my mother taught me how to make and bake bread. The aroma of loaves of bread lifted from the oven, making a good smell throughout the house."*

—Elizabeth Coblentz, 1993

The Amish are self-described "plain people," with a religion defined by simple dress, devout faith, and a desire to live unchanged by the touch of time. Amish churches are like snowflakes: There are no two exactly alike. And depending on which one you visit, you may feel like you stepped into a storybook where cars and computers are replaced by buggies and butter churns. The smell of homemade bread wafts from a wood-fired oven into the cold of a January afternoon. Or the sizzle of doughnuts being dropped into a pot of hot lard captivates children. While journeys to grocery stores—and even fast-food eateries—are becoming increasingly common for the Amish, they still aspire to live simply and self-sufficiently. An important element of this self-sufficiency comes through the culinary craft of baking.

The Old Order Amish, of which Lovina Eicher is a member, dress plainly: bonnets and solid-colored hand-sewn dresses for the women, hats and suspenders for the men. The Amish live in rural enclaves in over twenty-five states and Canada and are part of a larger Protestant religious movement known as the Anabaptists, which also include the Mennonites and Hutterites. Each practices its own unique brand of simplicity and piety. Anabaptism means "adult baptism." The Amish church was founded on the belief that children shouldn't be baptized because they don't yet have the maturity to choose their faith. Another hallmark of the Old Order

Amish is the practice of worshipping in their homes. The Old Order Amish do not have formal church buildings; instead services are held every other Sunday in the homes of congregants. While customs and church rules vary from community to community, most Old Order Amish still use horse-drawn buggies as their main mode of transport, and their homes are free from phones, electricity, and sometimes even indoor plumbing. Old Order Amish members, true to their European roots, are bilingual, speaking a dialect of German at home and English when interacting with those outside the faith. Non-Amish are often referred to as "English" or in some communities as "Yankees."

My initial taste of Amish-style baking was in a German Baptist home in rural southwest Ohio. The German Baptists are a religious group closely related to the Amish, and often mistaken for Amish because of their simple, plain dress. The Dunker faith originated from a later European religious movement known as Pietism. But the end result is a faith and lifestyle that share similarities to the Amish.

I was writing a story about the Dunkers for our local newspaper in my first job as a cub newspaper reporter for the *Middletown Journal*. After Sunday worship, two hours of beautiful, Gregorian chant–like singing and prayer, I was invited back to the minister's home, where we feasted on a lunch of baked chicken, green beans, homemade rolls, and fresh-baked chocolate cake. I felt awkward,

a seventeen-year-old journalism student sitting at a supper table with a group of much older strangers who looked as if they were torn from the pages of another era. But I was quickly won over by their warmth, kindness, and conversation. I felt a strong tug of fascination with these people and their seemingly simple way of life. I savored the goodness of the meal, the buttered, baked bread warm on my plate and the friendly fellowship warm on my heart. I was a typical teenager from the city, and these were pious people who made their living off the land. However, we seemed to bond over baked goods, and it was as if a bridge of fresh-baked bread was able to span the cultural and generational chasm separating us.

I remembered my mother telling me that her wedding cake was made by a German Baptist woman "out in the countryside" somewhere. And I had also sampled sourdough coffeecakes and cinnamon buns made by German Baptist bakers and sold at area farmers' markets. Growing up in southwest Ohio, I learned that there was something special about the soothing simplicity of plain baking.

It was journalism again that led me to my first taste of Amish baking. This time I received an assignment from a children's magazine to visit an Amish community. I was told to write a story in such a way that non-Amish students could learn and appreciate plain culture. I scoured the hills of southern Ohio looking for an Amish family that would be willing to open their home to me and teach me about their faith and culture. That's when I met the Keim family in rural Adams County, Ohio. The Keims ran, at the time, a small bakery situated along Ohio State Route 32, a winding ribbon of road that dips into the state's southern hill country. The Keim Family Market (see page 22) became a favorite place of mine during the weeks ahead, as I stopped in for cinnamon rolls and coffeecakes, and to learn about the Amish. As I gathered notes for my article, the Keims extended an invitation to come visit their home for supper, an invitation I eagerly accepted.

On a warm August evening with a chorus of crickets and tree frogs providing a summer symphony, we sipped ice-cold lemonade and munched on freshly baked buttered bread. It was a very pleasant supper enjoyed outside under a sprawling old oak. This was a land where power poles disappeared and the smoky-colored hills made the lights of nearby Cincinnati seem like a distant galaxy. As a new high-school graduate on the edge of adulthood, I again felt the powerful pull of what seemed like a lifestyle of simplicity and serenity. Like during that supper with the German Baptists a year earlier, I was connecting with my Amish hosts over fresh pie, bread, and baked chicken. Baked goods were again providing a common language, a shared love of fresh food, and a mutual appreciation of rhubarb pie. The smell of rhubarb would play a larger role at my next stop in Amish country.

### "THE AMISH BAKER?"

My deep appreciation for the basic goodness of Amish baking led me to believe that others, too, would enjoy a taste of the same simplicity I had experienced. So I decided that maybe I could find an Amish baker to write a weekly column about her fascinating food and culture. I visited various Amish communities, stopping at their bakeries and bulk-food stores in search of someone to pen this column. The full story is told in our first book, *The Amish Cook at Home,* but I was turned away by many would-be column writers. I think they viewed this young outsider with suspicion.

I was beginning to think that I was going to come up empty in my quest for an Amish columnist. But I thought I'd try one more place. There was an Amish-owned bakery deep in the Indiana countryside. Handwritten signs showed the way to Schwartz's Bakery. I thought maybe I'd find someone here to write the column. I entered the tiny bakery, by a weathered clapboard house, and was immediately struck by the wonderful smell of snickerdoodles, homemade pies, and handmade breads. This seemed promising.

But it was yet another dead end, because the owner said she was simply too busy to try such a thing. About to chalk up this idea to a youthful flight of insanity, I decided to head home. Unless I saw someone outside in their yard to talk to, I'd just give up on the idea. That's when just down the road from the bakery I saw a kindly, grandmotherly-looking Amish woman standing in her driveway. I've often asked myself how I ended up in Elizabeth Coblentz's driveway that summer afternoon. Was it fate steering me in a predetermined direction, or was it simply a lucky blunder? Either way, I had finally found "The Amish Cook."

As I pulled into Elizabeth Coblentz's homestead for the first time, I was immediately struck by the tart, tangy smell of rhubarb, a spring and summer staple in Amish kitchens. A small grove of apple trees

added a fruity fragrance to the July air. After a nervous introduction, I pitched the idea of writing a weekly recipe column to her, and she, without much hesitation, agreed to give it a try. During our visit Elizabeth offered me a taste of homemade rhubarb bread and some rhubarb pie. I was immediately enticed by the sour and sugary opposites in every bite. For Elizabeth, like many Amish, offering a slice of pie or homemade bread to a stranger is more than a simple act of kindness—it's extending a hand of friendship. So after less than half an hour, I went home for the first time with a loaf of homemade white bread and the beginning of a warm relationship that would last a lifetime.

I admit to struggling with names for what to call this weekly column. I thought for a long time about "The Amish Baker" or "Amish Diary." But in the end I settled upon "The Amish Cook," thinking the more expansive name described the column best. Elizabeth Coblentz wrote the column for eleven years, and now it is written by one of Elizabeth's daughters, Lovina Eicher. Lovina agreed to take over writing the column after her mother's sudden passing in 2002. Lovina lives in rural Michigan with her husband, Joe, and their eight children. Lovina's children often appear in the column, and they are, in order of oldest to youngest: Elizabeth, Susan, Verena, Benjamin, Loretta, Joseph, Lovina, and Kevin.

## WHO IS THE AMISH COOK?

Lovina writes about her life in her weekly syndicated column, "The Amish Cook." A typical column might describe a cozy winter's night in front of a coal stove piecing together puzzles and playing games; or a summer's afternoon spent in the garden, harvesting onions, tomatoes, and turnips; or baking bread and cookies for an upcoming church gathering. Old Order Amish conduct church services in their homes, not in a formal church building. Services are rotated among members, so each person usually hosts church once or twice a year. The weeks before church are always a blur of baking and cleaning. An excerpt from one of Lovina's writings before holding services gives a flavor for the column:

*"Morning chores are so much more pleasant with the barn all cleaned out now. The chicken coop looks nice and clean. We are getting anywhere from eight to twelve eggs a day, depending on the weather. When it gets colder they don't lay as much.*

*Meanwhile, I still had some leftover white curtain material from the last time I made new curtains. I was surprised that there was enough to make seven new curtains. My sister Emma took the material home and is sewing them for me. It really will assist me to have her sew the curtains. Emma, Verena, and Susan will also pitch in with baking loaves of white and wheat bread and cookies for church."*

While baking has often become back-burnered in our microwave and drive-through dinner world, a luxury reserved for retirement or a Christmas chore, for the Amish it's a necessity and also enjoyment. Mothers pass lessons learned to daughters over their first batch of brownies. Sisters who might see one another only once or twice a year renew bonds while baking bread before a wedding, their hands kneading dough in symphonic rhythm as if they've been playing together their whole lives.

## NOT ALONE

It didn't take me long to realize that I wasn't alone in my appreciation of the plain deliciousness of Amish baking. All it took was one bicycling trip to Lancaster County, Pennsylvania, when I was nineteen to see the millions of visitors who descend upon Amish country annually for a sampling of simplicity. And if you were to ask most of the visitors why, you might hear "for the simplicity," "for the pretty countryside," or the "beauty of the buggies," but, in reality, the biggest draw is probably the food. Amish bakeries turn out legendary confections like shoofly pie, funnel cakes, and soft pretzels. The main routes through Amish country are often full of kitschy, carnival-type vendors and gift shops featuring faceless Amish dolls and hex signs. Many of the roadside-stand souvenirs found here are for show. But

tucked away on rural homesteads, far from the trinkets and tourists, is the real deal: scratch-made cakes, homemade puffy pretzels (see page 78), and pies stuffed with hand-picked fruit filling. If one takes the time to travel the back roads, there are often Amish bakeries awaiting discovery. Hand-scrawled signs advertising "homemade pies" or "fresh-baked cookies" beckon. I've had soft-as-cotton-candy iced buttermilk cookies at a bakery in Nappanee, Indiana, cider doughnuts at an Amish orchard in Michigan, and apple fritters in Adams County, Ohio. Authentic Amish baking exists, but you have to stray from the main routes and explore the back roads to really get a taste.

## THE AMISH BAKER'S DOMAIN

An Amish kitchen isn't equipped with a Magic Bullet blender, a Cuisinart, or one of those cool countertop bread makers. An average Amish kitchen is packed with plenty of heavy-duty pots, pans, and hand-operated utensils. Since Amish hold their church services, weddings, and funerals at home, a kitchen must be equipped with more than enough hardware to feed the family, as it must feed the community on occasion. Lovina's kitchen (see Baking Tools, page 96) is typical of what is found in most Amish homes. The kitchen is wide and open to accommodate family members gathering, lunch-pail packing, and

plenty of baking. Some Amish light their homes with kerosene, others with gas. Lovina's house uses gas, so the kitchen ceiling is warmly lit with gaslights.

Amish cooks are voracious recipe swappers. When women gather at quilting bees, church services, and potlucks, they talk and trade new kitchen creations. Since Amish communities vary greatly in what is "allowable," recipes are often written in vague terms. For instance, some Amish settlements allow gas ovens. These give more reliable baking temperatures than kerosene or wood-fire ovens. So often Amish cooks will talk about a "hot oven" or a "slow oven." Recipes in this book have been adapted to include exact baking temperatures. But for cultural insight, here is a translation table:

**VERY SLOW OVEN:** 250° to 300°F

**SLOW OVEN:** 300° to 325°F

**MODERATE OVEN:** 325° to 375°F

**MEDIUM-HOT OVEN:** 375° to 400°F

**HOT OVEN:** 400° to 450°F

**VERY HOT OVEN:** 450° to 500°F

At first glance, Amish kitchens, most often, look surprisingly like any other kitchen. There are stainless steel or ceramic sinks. Lovina's mother's kitchen featured Formica countertops with stainless steel sinks. However, there was no faucet, and on more than one occasion I found myself wanting to put a dinner dish in the sink and grabbed for a hot water handle, only to find nothing. The Amish community she lived in did not allow indoor plumbing. The "faucet" was instead a hand-pump well located in a water closet off the kitchen. Oak cabinets with brass handles were underneath the counters. Elizabeth's kitchen was always spotlessly clean. Other Amish kitchens can be cluttered and chaotic, with large stainless steel pots hanging from hooks, baking sheets crammed into cabinets, and industrial-size vats for soups and stews that could feed a college football team. The kitchens reflect the personalities of the people in them.

Lovina's kitchen is L-shaped and open, with enough pots and pans neatly stored away to easily provide sustenance for a whole church district. Cookware is safely stowed, away from curious children who might find a large stainless steel stockpot a nice drum and a wooden spoon a drumstick. Lovina's refrigerator, gas stove, and Formica countertops add a twenty-first-century touch to a kitchen that otherwise looks much like one from the 1800s.

"Thinking big" is a common theme in Amish kitchens because so often a homemaker is called upon to serve voluminous quantities of food. In the event of a church service, wedding, funeral, barn-raising, or quilting bee, hundreds of people may need to be fed. And no Amish hostess worth her shoofly pie wants to be caught short. Even the Amish, though, may sometimes find that their duty to feed a crowd exceeds their ability. "Wedding wagons" (see page 195) are increasing in popularity among the Amish. These are "wedding-ready" contraptions with all the baking sheets, cake pans, soup vats, and salad bowls one would need for the 1,000 people who often show up at Amish weddings. Or sometimes, if the number of palates to please is overwhelming, an Amish cook will just throw in the towel and go to the grocery. On more than one occasion I found myself—and my car—pressed into service by Elizabeth to stop at the local wholesale bread store with a list that included 80 loaves of bread for upcoming church services.

The Amish are one of the last groups who still cling to the old ways of baking, viewing it still as more of an art and a pleasure than a chore. This book will serve as a primer for learning about the Amish, bite by tasty bite, through their baked goods. The following pages will be a journey through the baking culture of the Amish, through school events, weddings, and winters. There will also be a view of baking through the eyes of Lovina's children. Lovina is very typical of most Amish homemakers, raising a brood of children while also juggling mending, sewing, gardening, canning, helping with homework, and, yes, baking.

## BAKING EQUALS BONDING

Among the Amish, a loaf of homemade bread or a plate of homemade cookies can be the equivalent of a handshake or a hug. The Amish, true to their religious tenets of plainness, simplicity, and stoicism, have few outward ways in which they celebrate special occasions. Christmases are devoid of decorations, funerals free of flowers, and birthdays without confetti and clowns. One of the few ways in which the Amish do express themselves outwardly is through food. And baked goods occupy a central role in this Amish culinary and cultural emotional expression. Church is celebrated with cookies and coffeecakes, Christmas marked with fruitcakes and gingerbread, and weddings with cakes and pastries that are served only on this blessed occasion.

Amish baking is by its very definition simple, self-sufficient, and often sweet and sticky. The worn hands of an Amish homemaker kneading loaves of bread carry the lessons of generations past. There's a calming comfort in watching hands shape the dough, of watching bread balloon into a billowy golden pillow in a wood-fired oven. Throughout centuries of religious persecution in Europe and sometimes harsh settlement conditions in the United States and Canada, the Amish have turned to their hands to feed themselves: men to plant and harvest, women to bake and cook. This insular self-sufficiency has elevated the Amish into legendary creators of cakes, pies, rolls, and doughnuts out of the basic building blocks of baking: flour, eggs, butter, vanilla, oatmeal, seasonal fruits, cinnamon, and molasses.

Amish baking also often reflects the region of origin. Long before "eat local" became a trendy cultural and culinary catchphrase, the Amish were doing it out of necessity. The Amish of Maine load their coffeecakes with fresh wild blueberries in the summer, and the Amish-Mennonites in Georgia bake plump peaches into cookies and breads, while the Amish of Montana have perfected potato bread. Most all

Amish, though, especially those of the Midwest, Lovina's lineage, are bakers of scratch simplicity, using rhubarb, oatmeal, and molasses.

Baking is often considered a science, but among the Amish it's more often art. And art is sometimes subjective, inexact, and beholden to the artist's definition of beauty. Amish bakeries generally aren't steeped in science driven by the knowledge of how long yeast takes to ferment, exact water temperatures, and precise instructions. They instead are driven by experience and success passed between the generations. When comparing science-based baking to generational baking, one style of baking isn't better than the other, just different. Each produces its own successes. This book will share the Amish art of baking. We have tried to strike a balance between making the recipes as precise as possible and not stripping them of their Amish authenticity.

## FUNNY NAMES, GOOD FOOD

I once was eating dinner at Elizabeth Coblentz's house, and she served a salad to me and some guests that she simply called "Bob Salad."

"Looks good," I remarked. "Um, who's Bob?"

"I reckon I don't know," Elizabeth said, as we both pondered how some guy named Bob got a salad named after him. Flipping through the recipe boxes in any Amish kitchen will reveal a sometimes amusing hodgepodge of names for dishes. The Amish are such eager recipe swappers, traders, and adapters that unfortunately the origin of many of these recipe names has been lost in the passing. Among the Amish, baking is a bit like the "telephone game" (which is ironic, since most don't have phones) from grade school. A recipe gets passed, changed a bit, passed to someone else, changed yet again, and so on, so that the end result may not much resemble the original.

This book stays true to Amish traditions by keeping some of the original names, even though Lovina—and most Amish bakers—have long since lost the reason behind the names. Bob Andy Pie (page 7), Crybaby Cookies (page 113), Ranger Cookies (page 92), Shoofly Pie (page 43), Oatmeal Whoopie Pie Cookies (page 107), and the classic, Tears on Your Pillow Pie (page 17), are all names of baked goods found in the pages of this book. Another trait of Amish cooking is to be perhaps too honest in recipe names: Lard Cakes, Thick Milk Pie, and Vinegar Pie all appear on the follow pages. Lard cakes could be called "delicious doughnuts." And, in reality, the vinegar pie could be called "mock lemon pie" for its amazing resemblance to the fruit. Thick milk pie tastes quite a bit like pumpkin.

Lovina is in many ways a typical Amish homemaker. She faces the task each day of feeding a large family and balancing the needs of her children and husband, whether it be helping with homework, mending a dress, or tending to the garden. But somehow, despite all the chores and challenges, she still finds time to bake.

## BAKING WITH LOVINA

Baking is something my mother taught me, much like sewing, ironing, or gardening. Now, as a mother of eight children of my own, I am beginning to teach them how to bake. I have many cherished memories of baking throughout my life.

My mother was always doing a lot of baking in my growing-up years. As a child I would stand and watch her roll out pie dough and mix bread dough with her hands. She did have a hand-cranked bread mixer for doing larger batches. I had a craving to just stick my little hands in the dough and squeeze it. It amazed me how she could pick up the thinly rolled piecrusts and move them to the pie pans. Then she would do the crimping along the edges, her fingers moving very swiftly. I still cannot do the pie edges as fast and as perfectly as she did.

Mother would always set her bread dough on a chair by our coal stove to rise. The heat from the stove made it happen faster. In the summer months, when the stove wasn't going, she'd put the dough on a table where the sun would shine in. These are hints I use myself today as an adult. For instance, our coal stove is in the basement and our heat comes into the house through a large vent in the floor. Sometimes I set my dough on a step stool on top of the vent if I want it to rise faster. Or if I have my gaslights on I'll set my dough under the gaslight on the table. The gaslights throw off a lot of heat, so it helps the dough rise a lot faster.

Sometimes when I am rolling out pie dough or mixing up a batch of bread, I hear my daughters say, "Mom, how can you do that so fast?" Then I think maybe it is just a natural reaction because Mother seemed so perfect and did everything just right. Mother would give us the leftover dough after she had the amount needed for her pies. My sisters and I would use our toy rolling pins to roll out the dough and then ball it up and do it all over again. Then came the days when we were old enough to help with the baking.

Usually a cake was our first thing to do, followed by cookies, bars, and brownies. Then later we tried breads, rolls, and pies.

Since we moved to Michigan we have a gas stove. I soon learned that the gas stove heats up a lot faster than the kerosene ones we used in Indiana. I do prefer gas, as it seems to bake more evenly. I also feel safer letting my daughters bake with a gas oven. The kerosene burners would start smoking and the wicks needed to be kept clean so they would burn better. In the summer when windows were open, you had to make sure the wind didn't make the flame go up.

As a child, I would always be glad when I would see Mom start to do the Long John Rolls (page 183). They were a favorite of mine. She would roll out the dough and cut it into long pieces. After they would rise she would put them into hot lard and deep-fry them. After they were cooled she would put frosting on them. I would always like to see if I could pick out the longest one for myself. Now time has gone so fast and I'm teaching my own daughters how to bake. Most of my children have mixed together a cake. Even four-year-old Lovina and three-year-old Kevin have stirred the batter. Son Benjamin asked me if he could start learning to bake something other than a cake. I am glad when the children are interested in wanting to learn how to bake.

Baking can be a lot of fun, especially when you aren't rushing and pushed for time. I think one of my least favorite jobs is baking cookies, which explains why I'm turning that job over to my daughters quite fast. I enjoyed doing it before I was a busy mother, but now with eight children to feed, when we bake cookies we usually need a few hundred or more if we want them to last awhile. I do have baking sheets that hold up to twenty cookies, which helps speed up the baking quite a bit. I'm not sure if I have a favorite in baking, but I lean more toward breads and rolls than pies. It took me a little while until I learned the knack of rolling out a thin pie dough, but with a little effort anyone can learn. To some of my sisters the pie dough came easier than doing the bread dough; it just depends on your preference. I use a different pie dough recipe than my mother did. I think everyone has a certain pie dough or bread recipe that they prefer and have more luck with.

In teaching my daughters how to bake, we have had our share of laughs. When daughter Elizabeth was around nine years old, she wanted to bake a cake all by herself. She came up to me and said, "Mom, the recipe says to put three whole eggs in it." She thought that since it asked for whole eggs it must mean the shell and everything. She wanted to come check with me because she had never seen me put in whole eggs. I explained to her that sometimes the recipe will call for just egg whites or egg yolks.

Another time, when daughter Susan mixed some chocolate chip bars (see page 164), she misread the recipe. The recipe asked for a teaspoon of vinegar and she misread it and put in a cup of vinegar. I saw that the batter looked too thin, so I asked her how much of each ingredient she put in. I noticed that the 1-cup measurement looked like it had vinegar in it. Needless to say, we tossed that batter and mixed up another.

Certainly the boys and men can create some laughs too with baking. On my son Kevin's third birthday, I put his cake out on the back porch thinking it would be safe there. While Elizabeth and I were doing laundry, Kevin discovered his birthday cake. He came down to the basement where we were washing clothes. He was covered all over in chocolate frosting. He had mostly enjoyed the frosting and left the cake.

My husband Joe hardly ever does any baking—he'd rather do grilling or frying. One time when I was running short on time, he took over mixing some cake batter for me. I was busy doing other things and forgot that he was mixing the cake. Finally he asked me

I like to buy a lot of my ingredients at a bulk-food store since there are bigger sizes of everything. I always buy my bread flour in 25-pound bags. Brown sugar, powdered sugar, and oatmeal are more things that I like to buy in bulk. There are Amish-owned bulk-food stores in most communities. Buying in bulk is a great way to save money and is necessary when feeding a family of ten.

When you buy such huge amounts, a good way to store everything is in sealable containers. Any container that has a tight seal and will prevent ingredients from getting buggy will work. During the summer months bugs seem to be worse. I also put my spices in sealable containers to help prevent bugs. I have a set of stackable and sealable containers that fit nicely into my cabinet.

Lard is one ingredient I find myself buying less frequently. We always used lard when I was growing up, and I also used it up until a few years ago. We'd make our own lard every year when we butchered pigs. This lard would usually last from one year to the next. I have changed over to using vegetable shortening more instead of lard. A lot of people still use lard, and it can be used to make homemade soap. I cannot tell the difference in the flavor of piecrusts baked with lard or shortening. Mother always would use lard to fry anything, and so did I until I switched to butter and olive oil.

When the rhubarb is ready to use in the spring, Joe always asks me when I am going to make rhubarb pie. Rhubarb-custard (see page 30) and pecan (see page 38) are his favorite pies. Rhubarb-custard pie is also my favorite. Joe is always also glad when I make cinnamon rolls. If I haven't made cinnamon rolls for a while, he'll ask me when I am going to make some again. Chocolate chip cookies are Joe's favorite cookie, and he also really likes a frosted sugar cookie. I pack his lunch when he goes to work, and he always enjoys chocolate chip or sugar cookies in his bucket.

Joe's good sense of humor about baking reminds me of my father's. I remember when my sisters and I were still at home, Dad would always like chocolate chip cookies. Dad was a quiet man but

how long he had to keep mixing the cake batter. I felt bad that I had completely forgotten to tell him how long and there he was twenty minutes later, still stirring. It turned out to be one of the best, moistest cakes I have ever tasted. Joe says it is probably because he mixed it for such a long time.

## PREPARING TO BAKE

I always tell my daughters to get out all the ingredients before mixing something together. I learned my lesson too many times when I ran out of something or didn't have an item on hand. I try to keep a list on my refrigerator to jot down an ingredient if I am getting low. Usually when I run out of something I have been able to borrow from a neighbor. One time I ran out of cinnamon in the middle of making cinnamon rolls. Luckily, a neighbor-lady had some I could borrow.

he had a big sense of humor. He'd tease us when he ate our cookies that he was glad he had shoes on because if he dropped a cookie he would break a toe. He'd also tease us about having a tooth loose because he ate our cookies. It was all in fun and we knew he was just joking; our cookies were soft and yummy, but he teased us that they were hard and heavy. One time, though, his joke backfired on him when one of my sisters-in-law brought cookies. Dad thought one of his daughters made them and cracked the joke about not letting one of the cookies fall on his toes. I think Dad was more embarrassed than my sister-in-law was.

In this book we try to use simpler recipes that usually take ingredients that most cooks keep on hand. I hope you will all enjoy this baking book. I do hope it will be a big help in your kitchen. I thank our Heavenly Father for letting me grow up with a mother who not only taught me how to bake but also how to sew, clean, do laundry, and so on. And most of all I am thankful that my parents taught me to accept Jesus Christ as my savior. May God bless you all as you try out these recipes.

L.E.

# Chapter One

*"A pound of patience you must find, mix well with loving words so kind.*
*Drop 2 pounds of helpful deeds and thoughts of other peoples' needs.*
*A pack of smiles to make the crust. then stir and bake well you must.*
*And now I ask that you must try the recipe of this sunshine pie."*

— AUTHOR UNKNOWN

Perhaps no food symbolizes Amish culture more than pie. When many people envision Amish baking, a homemade piecrust bursting with fruit filling or billowy meringue is one of their first thoughts. A pie recipe was included in the very first "Amish Cook" column penned by Lovina's mother, Elizabeth Coblentz, in 1991. That recipe for Oatmeal Pie (page 194) is an old one that captures the creative cookery found in Amish kitchens. Oatmeal pie is a skillfully blended confection that creates an elegant dessert, but uses only the most basic ingredients.

Among the Amish, pie is more than just a sweet dessert. Meat and vegetable pies can make a meal. Raisin pies and oatmeal pies are special dishes served to mark the most meaningful ceremonies of life. Some pies are even enjoyed for breakfast. And perhaps, first and foremost, pies are simple ways to capture the seasonal and regional goodness of an area. In spring, strawberries and peaches are packed into the cozy confines of a homemade crust. Come June and July, pies capture the summer sweetness of berries, the sour of rhubarb, and even the savory of Zucchini Pie (page 39). When autumn comes, it is all apple or pumpkin. And the versatile pie is an easy way to feed a sweet snack to sudden company.

Outsiders have come to associate good pie—quality crust and thick fruit filling—with Amish baking. At Yoder's restaurant in the Amish enclave of Pinecraft, Florida, customers choose from twenty-eight flavors of pies on the menu throughout the year. "Peach is our most popular flavor," says Todd Emrich, general manager of Yoder's. Yoder's, opened by Mennonites in the 1970s, acts as a central gathering place in the local Amish community.

In one of California's lone "plain communities," a German Baptist bakery advertises "mile high pies." The pie is a massive confection made using 12 cups of apples. And in Missouri's Mennonite community, back-road bakeries tout their Show-Me-State pies with crusts carefully crafted by hand.

Like most Amish cooks, some of Lovina's earliest baking lessons revolve around that quest for the perfect pie, an experience she shares willingly.

## LOVINA'S PIES

I can still remember very well my first attempt at making pie. While growing up, I would watch my mother make pies time and time again. It looked so easy to do. That is probably why I was so frustrated when, as a young, just-married homemaker, I mixed up my first batch of pie dough. Everything was fine until I started rolling out the dough. The dough would just stick to my rolling pin. I kept adding flour but I could just not get the hang of it. Mother wasn't there so I couldn't ask her what to do. Finally I just gave up. It was quite awhile before I attempted it again, but this time with a crust recipe that that really seemed to work well (see My Homemade Pie Dough on page 3). I made a nice-looking cherry pie with this recipe. The lattice top even turned out perfect.

After that I had the urge to try it again. I always think once the dough is done then mixing the ingredients for the pie is easy. The baking part can be tricky, though. I remember when I put that first pie in the oven that the recipe said, "bake until done." (Editor's note: "Bake until done" is a common refrain in Amish kitchens, but with such a variety of stoves—wood, coal, and kerosene—pinning down baking times can be nearly impossible.) I baked it until I thought it was done. It looked like a very nicely shaped pumpkin pie. After it started cooling off, though, it sunk down in the middle. Mother told me it needed more baking time. I think it works best to put a cream or a pumpkin pie in the oven at a higher heat for the first 10 or 15 minutes and then reduce the heat. I always think with baking, experience is the best teacher.

I'll share a funny story about a local Amish man and his wife. They were attending a family Christmas gathering. The wife was taking some pies in a covered pie carrier. While loading up everything else, her husband placed the pie carrier on top of their covered buggy. He forgot he set it there and climbed in, and they drove four or five miles down some dirt roads and small hills. When they reached their destination their pies were still on the roof of their buggy, although the container had slid to the other side. Everyone enjoyed the still-perfect pies.

When I am transporting baked goods in the buggy, I usually put everything in a bag and slide it under the seat. One time when we were bringing home glass jars of milk, they tipped over in the buggy and broke. That was a big mess.

Pies are favorites at family gatherings, but they are also served on special occasions after church services. Several varieties of pies are served, usually three or four different kinds. The kinds of pies are usually chosen by the host. Some pies, such as cherry, raisin, apple, and gooseberry, look better with a lattice top. Other flavors, like Bob Andy Pie (page 7) and Oatmeal Pie (page 194) wouldn't look good with a lattice top. There are many kinds of lattice tops that can be used also. I have a lattice top that probably is one of the most popular, consisting of squares. But I also have one that has apple shapes. Some still do it the old-fashioned way with crisscrossing of the strips of dough.

Lattice-top pies make a pretty dessert on the table top. I always enjoyed watching Mother when I was younger making the lattice top. I'd ask her if I could poke out all the little pieces of dough. Mother taught me that when you put on a lattice top, you need to wet the rim of the bottom so that the two crusts will stay together without parting.

Pie sizes seem to have gradually changed. Mom would always make 8-inch pies when I was growing up, and that is what I started out making also. Now I hardly ever make 8-inch pies; I always do the 9-inch size. That one just serves more people, and that is now the size of pies you see served at wedding meals.

## MY HOMEMADE PIE DOUGH

### Makes 3 single 9-inch crusts

*No matter how good the filling of a pie, if the crust doesn't taste good the whole thing can be ruined. I have had luck with two different piecrust recipes. Don't get discouraged if you don't have success the first time. Sometimes you have to try a few times to get the experience.*

3 cups all-purpose flour
1 teaspoon salt
1 cup lard
1 large egg
⅓ cup cold water
1 tablespoon apple cider vinegar

In a large bowl, combine the flour and salt. Stir to blend. Add the lard and rub it into the flour with your fingertips until the mixture resembles coarse crumbs. Add the egg, water, and vinegar and stir with a fork until the dry ingredients are moistened. Form the dough into a ball and divide that into 3 balls. Form a ball into a disk and roll it out to a ⅛-inch thickness on a floured surface.

Fit the dough into a 9-inch pie pan and trim the edges to a 1-inch overhang. Fold the dough under and crimp the edges. If not using now, form the remaining 2 balls of dough into disks, place each in a resealable plastic bag, and freeze for up to 3 months.

## PAT-A-PAN PIECRUST

**Makes 1 single 9-inch crust**

*This is a great one to teach children to make a pie dough for the first time, or just for someone who is in a hurry and doesn't have time to roll out a crust. I think this tastes very good and works for a single-crust pie. The crust is quick and crisp and needs no rolling out. You cannot double this recipe or roll out a top crust, for it is just too tender to transfer from a pastry board to a pie tin. I recommend this recipe especially if you think you can't make a piecrust.*

1½ cups all-purpose flour

1½ teaspoons sugar

½ teaspoon salt

½ cup vegetable oil

3 tablespoons cold milk

Place the flour, sugar, and salt in a 9-inch pie pan and mix with your fingertips until evenly blended. In a measuring cup, combine the oil and milk and beat until creamy. Pour all at once over the flour mixture. Mix with a fork until the flour mixture is completely moistened. Pat the dough with your fingers, first at the sides of the plate and then across the bottom. Flute the edges.

The shell is now ready to be filled. If you are preparing a shell to fill later or your recipe requires a prebaked crust, preheat the oven to 425°F. Prick the surface of the pastry with a fork and bake until golden brown, 15 minutes. Check often and prick more if needed.

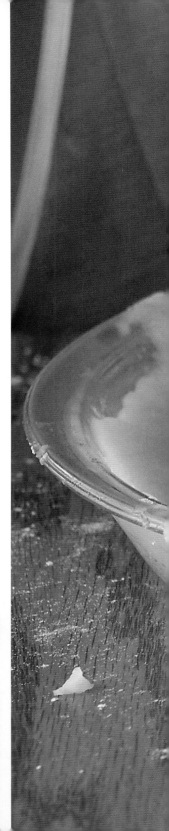

## "PLAIN PIES"

The first recipes in this chapter are traditional, simple recipes, most of which have been around for generations and have deep roots in the Amish community. Times were often tough and food scarce for the Amish in their early years in the United States. Fruit-filled pies were often a luxury. The following pie recipes are ones that can be made from scratch using the most basic ingredients, but the results are wonderful, with flavor surprising for such simplicity.

## CHOCOLATE CHIP PIE
### Makes one 9-inch pie

*If your children like chocolate chip cookies, then they'll love this pie. The dessert looks like a pie from the top, but when you cut into it, the inside resembles a chocolate chip cookie. A glass of cold milk goes great with a slice of this pie.*

1 disk My Homemade Pie Dough (page 3) or Pat-a-Pan Piecrust (page 4)
1 cup sugar
½ cup all-purpose flour
2 large eggs
½ cup melted butter
1½ cups semisweet chocolate chips
1 teaspoon vanilla extract

Preheat the oven to 350°F.

**For the homemade pie dough crust:** Roll the disk of pie dough out to a ⅛-inch thickness on a floured surface. Fit the dough into a 9-inch pie pan. Trim the overhang to 1 inch. Fold the dough under and crimp the edges.

**For the pat-a-pan piecrust:** Pat the dough with your fingers, first at the sides of the 9-inch pie pan and then across the bottom. Flute the edges.

In a large bowl, combine the sugar and flour; stir in eggs and butter until the batter is well-blended and smooth. Add the chocolate chips and vanilla extract; mix until smooth and the chocolate chips are evenly distributed. Pour the mixture into the unbaked pie shell. Bake at 350°F until golden brown, 40 to 45 minutes. Cool on a wire rack or windowsill until the pie is firm, about 45 minutes. Store any leftovers in a sealed cake safe. The pie will keep for about 5 days.

## BOB ANDY PIE

### Makes one 9-inch pie

*This favorite pie among the Amish can best be described as a "sweet custard." The cinnamon and cloves add a splash of spice and contribute to a dark, rich color. The pie's unusual name seems to have no shortage of stories about its origin. The most common tale is that an Amish farmer christened his wife's sweet concoction after their two prized geldings, who were named Bob and Andy. The pie seems to be especially favored by the Amish of Indiana and Illinois.*

1 disk My Homemade Pie Dough (page 3) or Pat-a-Pan Piecrust (page 4)

2 cups sugar

3 heaping tablespoons all-purpose flour

½ teaspoon ground cloves

1 teaspoon ground cinnamon

3 large eggs, separated

1 tablespoon butter, melted

2 cups milk

Preheat the oven to 350°F.

**For the homemade pie dough crust:** Roll the disk of dough out to a ⅛-inch thickness on a floured surface. Fit the dough into a 9-inch pie pan. Trim the overhang to 1 inch. Fold the dough under and crimp the edges.

**For the unbaked pat-a-pan piecrust:** Pat the dough with your fingers, first at the sides of the 9-inch pie pan and then across the bottom. Flute the edges.

In a large bowl, mix together the sugar, flour, cloves, and cinnamon. In a small bowl, beat the egg yolks. Then add the butter, yolks, and milk to the flour mixture and stir vigorously until the filling is creamy and light colored. In another separate small bowl, beat the egg whites for 2 minutes, until stiff peaks form, and then fold into the filling mixture. Pour the pie filling into the unbaked piecrust and bake for about 1 hour or until a butter knife inserted in the center comes out clean and the filling looks firm. Let set for about an hour before serving.

## CHOCOLATE NUT PIE
### Makes one 9-inch pie

*Most of the time the children don't like nuts in their dessert, but this pie is an exception. When I make this pie, it doesn't last very long around here! My daughter Susan is my "pie eater," because she seems to likes pie more than the other children, and she gave this pie her absolute approval.*

1 disk My Homemade Pie Dough (page 3) or Pat-a-Pan Piecrust (page 4)

½ cup margarine

¾ cup semisweet chocolate chips

3 large eggs

1 cup sugar

1 teaspoon vanilla extract

¾ cup walnuts

Preheat the oven to 350°F.

**For the homemade pie dough crust:** Roll the disk of pie dough out to an ⅛-inch thickness on a floured surface. Fit the dough into a 9-inch pie pan. Trim the overhang to 1 inch. Fold the dough under and crimp the edges.

**For the pat-a-pan piecrust:** Pat the dough with your fingers, first at the sides of the 9-inch pie pan and then across the bottom. Flute the edges.

Melt the margarine in a small saucepan over low heat. Add the chocolate chips to the margarine, stirring until melted. Remove from the heat and transfer to a large bowl. In a small bowl, beat the eggs lightly with a fork. Then stir the sugar, eggs, vanilla, and nuts into the chocolate mixture. Pour into the unbaked pie shell. Bake until the center is firm, about 45 minutes. While it bakes, the nuts will rise to the top. Cool on a wire rack or windowsill until the pie is firm, about 45 minutes. Store any leftovers in a sealed cake safe. The pie will keep for about 5 days.

## VINEGAR PIE

### Makes one 9-inch pie

*This is an old recipe with roots in the Great Depression, when years were lean and times were tough. Lemons and other fruits were often in short supply during the 1930s, so Amish homemakers turned to this recipe to make something that tastes and looks like a creamy lemon pie. A family in our church district has an apple orchard, and they make many gallons of cider but they also make apple cider vinegar. I have bought a lot of vinegar through the canning season.*

1 disk My Homemade Pie Dough (page 3) or Pat-a-Pan Piecrust (page 4)
½ cup (1 stick) butter, softened
1¼ cups sugar
2 tablespoons apple cider vinegar
3 large eggs
1 teaspoon vanilla extract

Preheat the oven to 350°F.

**For the homemade pie dough crust:** Roll the disk of pie dough out to an ⅛-inch thickness on a floured surface. Fit the dough into a 9-inch pie pan. Trim the overhang to 1 inch. Fold the dough under and crimp the edges.

**For the pat-a-pan piecrust:** Pat the dough with your fingers, first at the sides of the 9-inch pie pan and then across the bottom. Flute the edges.

In a large bowl, blend the butter and sugar until light and fluffy, about 2 minutes, stirring vigorously with a fork. Add the vinegar, eggs, and vanilla. Whisk vigorously for 1 full minute, until the mixture is creamy and smooth. Pour into the unbaked piecrust. Bake until a butter knife inserted in the center comes out clean, about 45 minutes. The pie will be a golden brown when done; overbaking will cause cracks in the top. Cool on a wire rack or windowsill until the pie is firm, about 45 minutes. This pie stays fresh for 3 days and should be stored in a sealed cake safe.

## VANILLA CRUMB PIE
### Makes one 9-inch pie

*With its crumb top, this pie has a crunchy top layer with a custard-like filling beneath. My daughter Elizabeth likes custard pie, and she says the filling of this pie reminds her of that. This is a very easy pie to make and tastes good served warm.*

1 disk My Homemade Pie Dough (page 3) or Pat-a-Pan Piecrust (page 4)

BOTTOM LAYER:
½ cup packed brown sugar
½ cup corn syrup
1 tablespoon all-purpose flour
1 large egg
1 cup water
1 teaspoon vanilla extract

TOP LAYER:
1 cup all-purpose flour
½ cup granulated sugar
¼ cup margarine
½ teaspoon baking soda
½ teaspoon baking powder

Preheat the oven to 375°F.

**For the homemade pie dough crust:** Roll the disk of pie dough out to ⅛-inch thickness on a floured surface. Fit the dough into a 9-inch pie pan. Trim the overhang to 1 inch. Fold the dough under and crimp the edges.

**For the pat-a-pan piecrust:** Pat the dough with your fingers, first at the sides of the 9-inch pie pan and then across the bottom. Flute the edges.

**To make the bottom layer:** In a medium saucepan, combine all the ingredients and cook over low heat, stirring, until thickened. Then pour into the unbaked pie shell.

**To make the top layer:** In a medium bowl, combine all the ingredients. Mix until coarse crumbs form. Distribute the crumbs evenly over the top of the filling. Bake until the crumbs on top get golden brown, 45 to 50 minutes. Cool on a wire rack or windowsill until the pie is firm, about 45 minutes. Store any leftovers in a sealed cake safe. The pie will keep for about 5 days.

## SAWDUST PIE

### Makes one 9-inch pie

*This pie's name is probably taken from the sawdust-like appearance of the pie, as sawdust is a familiar sight in Amish-owned mills and lumber-yards. This is a thick pie full of coconut.*

1 disk My Homemade Pie Dough (page 3)
    or Pat-a-Pan Piecrust (page 4)
1½ cups shredded coconut
1½ cup graham cracker crumbs
1½ cup chopped pecans
1½ cups sugar
1 cup egg whites (4 to 5 egg whites)

Preheat the oven to 350°F.

**For the homemade pie dough crust:** Roll the disk of pie dough out to a ⅛-inch thickness on a floured surface. Fit the dough into a 9-inch pie pan. Trim the overhang to 1 inch. Fold the dough under and crimp the edges.

**For the pat-a-pan piecrust:** Pat the dough with your fingers, first at the sides of the 9-inch pie pan and then across the bottom. Flute the edges.

In a medium bowl, combine the coconut, graham cracker crumbs, pecans, and sugar. Mix in the egg whites (do not beat them first). Pour the filling into the unbaked pie shell. Bake for 35 to 40 minutes. The middle may still look moist, but it will set upon cooling. Cover the edges only with foil if needed to prevent over-browning. Cool on a wire rack or windowsill until the pie is firm, about 45 minutes. Store any leftovers in a sealed cake safe. The pie will keep for about 3 days.

## HOMEMADE BUTTERMILK PIE

**Makes one 9-inch pie**

*In the community where we live in Michigan, Amish farmers are allowed to have bulk tanks for their milk. I was raised in a community where we kept the milk in cans. Having milkers and a bulk tank allows the Amish farmers to have many more cows. A farmer who has to milk his cows by hand can't have as many cows. There are other ways that milk can be used besides for drinking and cooking. I remember Mom making our own cottage cheese. When she would make butter, she would skim off the top layer of cream from the milk. Since we didn't have a butter churn, the children's job was to keep shaking the glass jar until the butter formed. Mom would then take out the lump of butter, and the liquid left was buttermilk. This recipe makes a warm, golden-colored pie that can be enjoyed as a dessert, with breakfast, or as a snack.*

1 disk My Homemade Pie Dough (page 3) or Pat-a-Pan Piecrust (page 4)

½ cup (1 stick) butter, softened

1 cup fresh buttermilk

3 large eggs

1½ cups sugar

1 tablespoon all-purpose flour

1 teaspoon ground nutmeg

Preheat the oven to 350°F.

**For the homemade pie dough crust:** Roll the disk of pie dough out to an ⅛-inch thickness on a floured surface. Fit the dough into a 9-inch pie pan. Trim the overhang to 1 inch. Fold the dough under and crimp the edges.

**For the pat-a-pan piecrust:** Pat the dough with your fingers, first at the sides of the 9-inch pie pan and then across the bottom. Flute the edges.

In a large bowl, beat together the butter, buttermilk, eggs, sugar, and flour with a whisk. Pour the filling into the unbaked piecrust. Sprinkle the top with the nutmeg. Bake until the pie turns a golden brown color and a butter knife inserted in the center comes out clean, about 35 minutes. Cool on a wire rack or windowsill until the pie is firm, about 45 minutes. Store any leftovers in a sealed cake safe. The pie will keep for about 2 days.

## SUGAR CREAM PIE

### Makes one 9-inch pie

*This is an old favorite among Amish in the Midwest. The pie is made from simple staples found in most peoples' pantries. While there are many local variations in sugar cream pie recipes, this one is very typical of what is served most often. My children like it because it tastes kind of like a sweet pudding.*

1 disk My Homemade Pie Dough (page 3) or Pat-a-Pan Piecrust (page 4)

½ cup granulated sugar

⅓ cup packed brown sugar

¼ cup all-purpose flour

¼ teaspoon salt

½ cup boiling water

½ cup thin cream or half-and-half

½ teaspoon vanilla extract

¼ teaspoon ground nutmeg

Preheat the oven to 425°F.

**For the homemade pie dough crust:** Roll the disk of pie dough out to a ⅛-inch thickness on a floured surface. Fit the dough into a 9-inch pie pan. Trim the overhang to 1 inch. Fold the dough under and crimp the edges.

**For the pat-a-pan piecrust:** Pat the dough with your fingers, first at the sides of the 9-inch pie pan and then across the bottom. Flute the edges.

In a large bowl, combine the sugars, flour, and salt until well blended. Slowly add the boiling water and stir until well blended. Then add the cream, vanilla, and nutmeg and stir until the mixture is completely blended. Pour the filling into the unbaked pie shell. Bake for 20 minutes. Reduce the oven temperature to 350°F and bake for 20 to 25 minutes more, until done. The top should be lightly bubbling all over and no longer liquid, but it should still jiggle like gelatin in the center. Let cool before serving. Cool on a wire rack or windowsill until the pie is firm, about 45 minutes. Store any leftovers in a sealed cake safe. The pie will keep for about 5 days.

## TEARS ON YOUR PILLOW PIE

### Makes one 9-inch pie

*The origins of this pie's funny name are unknown. No one I know seems to remember where its name comes from. My editor tells me that if you remove the pie from the oven too early it will collapse, which could cause bakers to head to bed with tears on their pillow. He also said that someone told him that the pie tasted so soft inside that it was like a pillow.*

1 disk My Homemade Pie Dough (page 3) or Pat-a-Pan Piecrust (page 4)

⅓ cup butter, melted

1½ cups packed brown sugar

2 large eggs

1 tablespoon all-purpose flour

½ cup evaporated milk

Preheat the oven to 350°F.

**For the homemade pie dough crust:** Roll the disk of pie dough out to a ⅛-inch thickness on a floured surface. Fit the dough into a 9-inch pie pan. Trim the overhang to 1 inch. Fold the dough under and crimp the edges.

**For the pat-a-pan piecrust:** Pat the dough with your fingers, first at the sides of the 9-inch pie pan and then across the bottom. Flute the edges.

In a large bowl, beat together the butter, brown sugar, eggs, flour, and milk until smooth. Pour the filling into the unbaked pie shell. Bake for 25 minutes or until the crust and filling are golden brown. Turn off the oven and leave the pie in the closed oven for 1 hour, and then remove it. This pie should be eaten within a day or two of baking.

**BAKING TIP:**
To soften brown sugar that has hardened, put the sugar in a sealed container with a slice of bread. After a couple of hours, remove the bread and the sugar will be softened.

## CORNMEAL PIE
**Makes one 9-inch pie**

*This is a very moist pie that tastes a bit like sweet cornbread in a piecrust. Be sure not to bake it too long or the top will develop cracks. People who like soft and sweet cornbread will really enjoy this pie.*

1 disk My Homemade Pie Dough (page 3) or Pat-a-Pan Piecrust (page 4)

2 large eggs

1½ cups packed brown sugar

3 tablespoons butter, softened

¼ cup heavy whipping cream

2 tablespoons cornmeal

Preheat the oven to 300°F.

**For the homemade pie dough crust:** Roll the disk of pie dough out to a ⅛-inch thickness on a floured surface. Fit the dough into a 9-inch pie pan. Trim the overhang to 1 inch. Fold the dough under and crimp the edges.

**For the pat-a-pan piecrust:** Pat the dough with your fingers, first at the sides of the 9-inch pie pan and then across the bottom. Flute the edges.

In a small bowl, beat the eggs and set aside. In a large bowl, stir the brown sugar, butter, cream, and cornmeal together until evenly blended. Then stir in the eggs, mixing vigorously until the mixture is smooth. Pour into the unbaked piecrust and bake until the center is set, 35 to 40 minutes. Cool on a wire rack or windowsill until the pie is firm, about 45 minutes. Store any leftovers in a sealed cake safe. The pie will keep for about 3 days.

## THICK MILK PIE
### Makes one 9-inch pie

*This pie's name doesn't sound appetizing, but it is a very delicious, economical pie to make. This is a great pie to make if you happen to have milk that has gone sour. Surprisingly, it tastes a little like pumpkin pie. The pie will not look set when taken out of the oven. It will look like pools of liquid, but will set once it cools. Molasses can be used in place of the honey (see table, page 197).*

1 disk My Homemade Pie Dough (page 3) or Pat-a-Pan Piecrust (page 4)

3 large eggs

1 cup honey

1 cup sugar

½ cup all-purpose flour

1 teaspoon baking soda

3 cups thick, sour milk or buttermilk (page 59)

2 teaspoons ground cinnamon

Preheat the oven to 400°F.

**For the homemade pie dough crust:** Roll the disk of pie dough out to a ⅛-inch thickness on a floured surface. Fit the dough into a 9-inch pie pan. Trim the overhang to 1 inch. Fold the dough under and crimp the edges.

**For the pat a pan piecrust:** Pat the dough with your fingers, first at the sides of the 9-inch pie pan and then across the bottom. Flute the edges.

In a large bowl, beat the eggs and add the honey. Combine the sugar, flour, and baking soda with the egg mixture. Add the thick milk and stir until smooth. Pour into the unbaked pie shell. Sprinkle the cinnamon over the top. Bake for 10 minutes. Then decrease the heat to 325°F and bake for 45 to 50 more minutes, or until a toothpick comes out clean. Cool on a wire rack or windowsill until the pie is firm, about 45 minutes. Store any leftovers in a sealed cake safe. The pie will keep for 2 days.

## BUTTERSCOTCH PIE

### Makes one 9-inch pie

*This is one of my brother Amos's favorite pies. My children also like it because they are fond of most cream pies. I don't think homemade butterscotch is difficult to make, and it will last a lot longer than the instant kind.*

1 disk My Homemade Pie Dough (page 3) or Pat-a-Pan Piecrust (page 4)

1 cup packed brown sugar

¼ teaspoon salt

2 cups boiling water

1 teaspoon vanilla extract

4 tablespoons (½ stick) butter, softened

2 large eggs

½ cup granulated sugar

Pinch of salt

1 cup all-purpose flour

1 cup milk

Preheat the oven to 350°F.

**For the homemade pie dough crust:** Roll the disk of pie dough out to a ⅛-inch thickness on a floured surface. Fit the dough into a 9-inch pie pan. Trim the overhang to 1 inch. Fold the dough under and crimp the edges. Bake the piecrust for 8 to 10 minutes, until golden. Remove from the oven.

**For the pat-a-pan piecrust:** Preheat the oven to 425°F. Pat the dough with your fingers, first at the sides of the 9-inch pie pan and then across the bottom. Flute the edges. Prick the surface of the pastry with a fork 3 times and bake until golden brown, 15 minutes.

In a small saucepan over low heat, boil the brown sugar, salt, water, vanilla, and butter. Mix until well blended, and then stir in the eggs, sugar, salt, flour, and milk. Cook, stirring, until thick, about 10 minutes. Pour into the baked piecrust and let cool to room temperature before serving.

# A VISIT TO AN AMISH BAKERY

Whether it is the Hillside Bakery in Arthur, Illinois; Mary's Amish Market in Pfeiffer Station, Ohio; or Chet & Beth's Amish Bakery in Choteau, Oklahoma, all have one thing in common: legions of fans.

But whether it's shoofly pie or cream horns that draw the masses, there seems to be something inherent in "Amish baking" that makes these mom-and-pop places such a draw. Dan Miller, the Amish owner of Keim Family Market in Seaman, Ohio, thinks he knows the answer, and it's a simple one.

"What makes the difference is that we make most of our stuff from scratch. There's just a difference in taste. When you use big equipment like on an assembly line, you lose the homemade flavor," he says.

The Keim Family Market was started in the mid-1980s by Roy and Mattie Keim after farming just proved too tough a way to support a family. Roy started selling baked goods and cheeses from his buggy. I can remember him pulling a block of cheese out of a Coleman cooler, a seemingly contradictory bow to modernity in the back of a buggy. People kept coming, and they still do, even though Roy and Mattie sold the bakery to Miller and moved to Michigan a year or so ago.

Miller is a genial, easygoing man with a long red beard and a good sense for what baked goods sell and which ones don't. Three items seem to occupy the top of the customers' list of favorites, which keep them coming back. "Cinnamon rolls, cream horns, and soft pretzels. Those three items pull people in time and time again," Miller says.

On a recent visit, my wife and I succumbed to the pull of the pretzel. We bought the big, doughy, soft treats and some sweet dipping mustard to go with them and had a lunchtime pretzel feast. I could see why people keep coming back.

Miller's lead baker, a recently married homemaker by the name of Naomi, calls fruitcake the most labor intensive item to make. "The decorating makes it the most time-consuming because it is all done by hand," she says.

The bakery seems to hold its own even with the fickle ups and downs of the American economy.

"I might not sell as many gazebos or big furniture items," Miller says, but, he adds, "People are going to eat, regardless."

Despite the hustle and bustle of the bakery and the seemingly modern swirl around him, Miller says the core of Amish life really remains intact. "Our lifestyle at home doesn't really change much," Miller says.

In another part of the state, much the same sentiments can be found at the Country Crust Bakery. The bakery is mistaken by most visitors as Amish-run.

"We're Old Order Mennonites," explains Luke Martin, owner of Country Crust. "No beards here with the men; otherwise we are very similar." The similarities extend to the baked goods. A crew of bonnet-clad women is whipping up coffeecakes, cream horns, pies, and pizzas in a tiny, but efficient, bakery. A large plate glass window behind the women opens to a snowy, sweeping vista of Ohio cornfield countryside. Country Crust Bakery is also known for handmade, homemade pumpkin rolls, doughnuts, and apple fritters.

A 60-gallon vat of white meringue sits ready to be poured onto pies. "Twice a week," one of the workers says, when asked how often they make the pie topping.

"Bread is the top seller here," Luke Martin says, "but we also move a lot of cookies."

So, what is Martin's assessment of why Amish and Mennonite bakeries enjoy such a public following? "The taste is the biggest thing. Making things from scratch and using quality ingredients make all the difference," Martin says. "Supermarkets use too many mixes and frozen items, and those just don't taste as good."

Lancaster County, Pennsylvania, was once home to the world's largest Amish community. But with such a large population came tourism, scrutiny, and simplicity-seeking suburbanites. So the weary Amish residents of Lancaster County began resettling in Wayne County, Indiana, during the mid-1990s. They've found the plentiful farmland and rural ways appealing, and the community has really taken root.

"There's just a little more elbow room out here," says a recent Amish transplant from Lancaster County.

As in most Amish communities, businesses such as dry-goods stores, bakeries, and harness shops have sprouted. The businesses serve Amish customers as well as English.

Fountain Acres Foods is a combination bakery and bulk-food store run by an Amish couple, Stevie and Marianne Miller. Fountain Acres churns out loaves of fluffy white and wheat bread, sweet cinnamon rolls, and whoopie pies. All the goodies are homemade from scratch, which Miller says is the key to Amish baking. "I think the reason people like Amish baking is that the girls are taught how to bake at a very early age using recipes that have been handed down through the generations," Stevie says.

In addition to the baked bread and whoopie pies, more unusual confections like Shoofly Pie (page 43) and a variety of bars are sold. Shoofly is a staple among the Amish of Pennsylvania, but Stevie Miller says it hasn't really caught on in Indiana. "But our black raspberry pies, our customers love those."

## FRUIT PIES

When harvests have been healthy and robust or economic times more prosperous, fruit pies have enjoyed popularity in Amish kitchens. There are fruit pie fillings harvested from "wild" sources, like gooseberries, mulberries, and raspberries, which can be gathered during Midwestern summers. There are also fruit pies that come from home harvests, like an apple orchard, strawberry patch, or peach tree.

## HOMEMADE FRUIT FILLINGS

My mother made a lot of her own homemade pie fillings, which were always delicious. She passed along many of her recipes and methods to her daughters. As a mother with a family of my own now, I have made strawberry, cherry, blueberry, and apple pie fillings from scratch. I've not tried making a peach pie filling yet, but I want to someday. The canned store-bought pie fillings taste okay, but I like the homemade ones better. I don't think Grandma would have ever bought a can of pie filling in the store. Back then they didn't even consider doing that. In later years, my mom might have bought a can at the store in a pinch. The look of homemade pie filling is different. The one you buy in the store probably looks nicer and the cherries are probably a little more red and plump. The cherries in homemade pie filling may seem more cooked. But the taste is better, I think.

I remember the first summer after my mother passed away, we started making homemade strawberry pie filling. I remember the first batch was too thick, so I tried a different recipe and it was good. We had such a supply of strawberries that year that I think we were so "strawberried out" by the time we got done working up all those berries that I was tired of that fruit for a while. But after we moved to Michigan I started my own strawberry patch, and we really enjoy these pie fillings again. Our whole family loves strawberries. I use these fillings not just for pies but also for puddings and other desserts.

It is great when you grow your own fruit because the fillings can be made at your own place. For example, my mother's homemade apple pie filling came from the apples on her trees. With my daughters getting out of school soon I'll have more help here at home, so I'll be able to do more of a variety. Making your own pie filling can be time-consuming, and extra hands make it go more quickly.

## FRUIT PIE FILLING
### Makes 3½ to 4 quarts of filling

*This recipe for homemade pie filling can be used for any fruit of your choice, including our favorite: strawberry. This filling recipe uses Perma-Flow, which is becoming popular among the Amish. A lot of us are going to Perma-Flow because it keeps the fruit filling nice and fresh over a period of years. If you don't get all your fruit filling used up in a season, it'll keep it for several years. It keeps the filling nice, and I can buy it at the bulk-food store.*

5 cups sugar

8 cups fruit, peeled, cored, and seeded as necessary

8 cups water

1¼ cups Perma-Flow

In a large bowl, add half of the sugar to the fruit and let stand overnight. The next day, drain the liquid from the fruit into another large bowl and add enough water to have 8 cups. Cook the Perma-Flow, the rest of the sugar, and the water together in a large pot for 10 minutes. Add the fruit and cook for another 10 minutes. Put into jars and cold pack (see below) for 10 minutes. This can be used for pie or cheesecake.

**Cold Packing:** Lovina and many Amish cooks use a method of canning known as "cold packing." This involves processing glass jars full of food by submerging them in a boiling water bath before sealing. The USDA no longer considers the "cold pack" method of canning safe, but many Amish still use the practice. Please consult the USDA's updated canning guidelines online or consult your local agricultural extension agent.

## BLUEBERRY PIE FILLING
### Makes 6 quarts

*This recipe is another great way to make pie filling. This is my recipe for blueberry filling, but you can substitute any fruit.*

6 cups sugar

2¼ cups instant Clear Gel

7 cups cold water

½ cup fresh lemon juice

6 quarts fresh blueberries or unsweetened frozen blueberries

In a large pot, combine the sugar and Clear Gel over medium-high heat. Add the water and stir. Cook on medium-high until the mixture thickens and begins to bubble, about 7 minutes. Add the lemon juice and boil for 1 more minute, stirring constantly. Fold in the berries, and then put into jars and cold pack. Store in a cool place. Use as pie filling.

## APRICOT PIE
### Makes one 9-inch pie

*Dried fruits and nuts are commonly sold in Amish-owned bulk-food stores. During tighter economic times, if fresh produce wasn't available, Amish cooks would often rely on the dried fruits sold in the bulk stores. This recipe has you plump up the dried apricots, which results in a very fruity pie. Some say this resembles a homemade peach pie.*

2 disks My Homemade Pie Dough (page 3)

2 cups dried apricots

2 cups water

½ cup sugar

1½ tablespoons cornstarch

Pinch of salt

3 tablespoons butter, cut into pieces

Preheat the oven to 425°F.

**For the homemade pie dough crust:** Roll both disks of pie dough out to a ⅛-inch thickness on a floured surface. Fit one of the dough disks into a 9-inch pie pan. Trim the overhang to be even with the top of the pie pan. Set the other rolled-out crust aside.

In a small saucepan, bring the apricots and the water to a boil. Cook for 10 minutes over low heat. Add the sugar and cook for another 5 minutes, stirring occasionally. Using a colander, drain the contents of the saucepan, reserving 1 cup of the juice. Set the apricots aside. Pour the reserved apricot juice into a small saucepan and add the cornstarch. Add the salt and cook over medium heat until the mixture thickens, 2 to 3 minutes, stirring frequently until the consistency is like gravy.

Arrange the drained apricots in the unbaked pie shell. Pour the thickened apricot juice over the apricots. Dot the top with the butter. Use some water to wet the rim of the bottom crust, which will help both crusts adhere together. Cover with the top crust and crimp the top and the bottom together all the way around. Slit the top 3 times and flute the edges. Bake for 30 minutes. Cover the edges only with foil, if needed, after 20 minutes, to prevent browning. Cool on a wire rack or windowsill until the pie is firm, about 45 minutes. Store any leftovers in a sealed cake safe. The pie will keep for about 5 days.

## RHUBARB-CUSTARD PIE
### Makes one 9-inch pie

*When the rhubarb begins peeping up on the first days of spring, this is a pie we often think of making first. And if someone's wedding falls during the summer, rhubarb-custard pie is often served. It was one of the pie flavors served at our wedding.*

1 disk My Homemade Pie Dough (page 3) or Pat-a-Pan Piecrust (page 4)

3 cups diced rhubarb

½ cup sugar

2 tablespoons cornstarch

¼ teaspoon salt

1 large egg

¾ cup corn syrup

1 tablespoon butter, softened

Preheat the oven to 450°F.

**For the homemade pie dough crust:** Roll the disk of pie dough out to a ⅛-inch thickness on a floured surface. Fit the dough into a 9-inch pie pan. Trim the overhang to 1 inch. Fold the dough under and crimp the edges.

**For the pat-a-pan piecrust:** Pat the dough with your fingers, first at the sides of the 9-inch pie pan and then across the bottom. Flute the edges.

Place the rhubarb in the unbaked pie shell. In a large bowl, combine the sugar, cornstarch, and salt. Add the egg and beat well. Then add the corn syrup and butter. Beat until smooth, and pour over the rhubarb. Bake for 15 minutes. Then decrease the heat to 350°F and bake for 30 more minutes or until the rhubarb is tender. Cool on a wire rack or windowsill until the pie is firm, about 45 minutes. Store any leftovers in a sealed cake safe. The pie will keep for about 5 days.

## SWISS CUSTARD PEACH PIE

Makes one 9-inch pie

*Fresh peaches are always a hit in my household. We like to use them in pies or sometimes in homemade preserves. This is an easy pie to make that is both pretty and tasty!*

1 disk My Homemade Pie Dough (page 3) or Pat-a-Pan Piecrust (page 4)

5 fresh peaches or 1 pint sliced peaches, drained

2 large eggs

½ cup sugar

¼ teaspoon salt

2 tablespoons butter, melted

1 (14-ounce) can sweetened condensed milk

Preheat the oven to 375°F.

**For the homemade pie dough crust:** Roll the disk of pie dough out to a ⅛-inch thickness on a floured surface. Fit the dough into a 9-inch pie pan. Trim the overhang to 1 inch. Fold the dough under and crimp the edges.

**For the pat-a-pan piecrust:** Pat the dough with your fingers, first at the sides of the 9-inch pie pan and then across the bottom. Flute the edges.

Place the peaches in the unbaked piecrust. Mix the eggs with the sugar, salt, and butter. Beat until well blended. Add the condensed milk. Beat once more until well blended. Pour the mixture over the peaches in the shell. Bake for 15 minutes. Decrease the heat to 300°F and bake for 40 to 50 minutes longer, until the custard is firm and no longer jiggles in the middle. Cool on a wire rack or windowsill until the pie is firm, about 45 minutes. Store any leftovers in a sealed cake safe. The pie will keep for about 3 days.

BAKING TIP:

I like to store fruit pies in the refrigerator. They usually last a week or a week and a half in the refrigerator. If you leave them out in the summertime, they don't last as long as they do in the wintertime.

## BUMBLEBERRY PIE

### Makes one 9-inch pie

*This is a delicious pie during the summer months. There's no such thing as a bumbleberry—it's just the name people give to this pie because it has all sorts of fruits in it. You can use whatever fruits are available or in season. Substitute seasonal fruits using the same amounts.*

2 disks My Homemade Pie Dough (page 3)
1 cup blueberries
1 cup raspberries
1 cup strawberries, chopped
1 cup chopped rhubarb
1 cup peeled and chopped McIntosh apples
1 cup sugar, plus more for topping
⅓ cup all-purpose flour
1 tablespoon fresh lemon juice

Preheat the oven to 425°F.

*For the homemade pie dough crust:* Roll both disks of pie dough out to a ⅛-inch thickness on a floured surface. Fit one of the dough disks into a 9-inch pie pan. Trim the overhang to be even with the top of the pie pan. Set the other rolled-out crust aside.

In a large bowl, combine all of the remaining ingredients until well blended. Spoon the fruit filling into the piecrust. Use some water to wet the rim of the bottom crust, which will help both crusts adhere together. Cover the pie with the top crust and crimp the crusts together all the way around. Make 3 slits in the crust. Sprinkle the top with a little sugar. Bake for 15 minutes, and then decrease the heat to 325°F and bake for another 30 minutes, until the crust is golden and the fruit filling begins to bubble out through the slits. Cool on a wire rack or windowsill until the pie is firm, about 45 minutes. Store any leftovers in a sealed cake safe. The pie will keep for about 5 days.

## GOOSEBERRY PIE

**Makes one 9-inch pie**

*Gooseberries can be difficult to find if they aren't in season. You can buy them in some stores, but mostly they are found growing in woods and meadows in the Midwest. Gooseberries also make a great jam or preserve*

2 disks My Homemade Pie Dough (page 3)

2 cups sugar

2 cups gooseberries

1 tablespoon all-purpose flour

Walnut-size pat of butter

Preheat the oven to 425°F.

**For the homemade pie dough crust:** Roll both disks of pie dough out to a ⅛-inch thickness on a floured surface. Fit one of the dough disks into a 9-inch pie pan. Trim the overhang to 1 inch. Fold the dough under and crimp the edges. Set the other rolled-out disk aside.

Put the sugar, berries, flour, and butter into a bowl and mix. Then pour into the pie shell. Use some water to wet the rim of the bottom crust, which will help both crusts adhere together. Cover the pie with the top crust, crimping the crusts together all the way around. Bake for 35 minutes or until the crust is golden brown. Cool on a wire rack or windowsill until the pie is firm, about 45 minutes. Store any leftovers in a sealed cake safe. The pie will keep for about 5 days.

## LEMON PIE

### Makes one 9-inch pie

*In the summertime I buy a lot of lemons, and I slice them and make my own lemonade. I like to eat the lemon slices, rind and everything. I remember my mom doing that also.*

1 disk My Homemade Pie Dough (page 3) or Pat-a-Pan Piecrust (page 4)

3 tablespoons cornstarch

1¼ cups plus 6 tablespoons sugar

¼ cup fresh lemon juice

1 tablespoon lemon zest

3 large eggs, separated

1½ cups boiling water

Preheat the oven to 425°F.

**For the homemade pie dough crust:** Roll the disk of pie dough out to a ⅛-inch thickness on a floured surface. Fit the dough into a 9-inch pie pan. Trim the overhang to 1 inch. Fold the dough under and crimp the edges.

**For the pat-a-pan piecrust:** Pat the dough with your fingers, first at the sides of the 9-inch pie pan and then across the bottom. Flute the edges.

In a medium bowl, combine the cornstarch, 1 ¼ cups sugar, the lemon juice, and lemon zest. In a small bowl, beat the egg yolks. Add the egg yolks to the cornstarch mixture. Gradually add the boiling water to the mixture, stirring all the while. Pour the mixture into a small saucepan and heat to boiling over medium heat. Boil gently for 4 minutes, stirring constantly. Pour into the unbaked pie shell. In a separate bowl, beat the egg whites until stiff, but not dry. Gradually beat in the remaining 6 tablespoons of sugar. Spread the meringue over the top of the pie. Bake for 5 to 10 minutes or until browned. Cool on a wire rack or windowsill until the pie is firm, about 45 minutes. Store any leftovers in a sealed cake safe. The pie will keep for about 5 days.

## MOTHER'S PLAIN APPLE PIE

**Makes one 9-inch pie**

*Mom would get the apples from her trees for homemade applesauce and apple pies. We had three apple trees on our property that were planted the year I was born. This helped my parents remember how old the trees were. When Mom would send us to go out to get apples, we had to go to certain trees. For the applesauce we used Yellow Transparent and for snacking, the Jonathan. Mom never measured anything for her apple pie; she always just knew how to make it perfect every time.*

1 disk My Homemade Pie Dough (page 3) or Pat-a-Pan Piecrust (page 4)
¾ cup granulated sugar
1 teaspoon ground cinnamon
6 to 7 cups sliced McIntosh apples
½ cup (1 stick) butter, softened
½ cup packed brown sugar
1 cup all-purpose flour

Preheat the oven to 425°F.

**For the homemade pie dough crust:** Roll the disk of pie dough out to a ⅛-inch thickness on a floured surface. Fit the dough into a 9-inch pie pan. Trim the overhang to 1 inch. Fold the dough under and crimp the edges.

**For the pat-a-pan piecrust:** Pat the dough with your fingers, first at the sides of the 9-inch pie pan and then across the bottom. Flute the edges.

Mix the sugar and cinnamon with the apples in a large bowl and put into the unbaked pie shell. Mix the butter, brown sugar, and flour in a medium bowl for the topping. Sprinkle over the pie. Bake for 15 minutes, then lower the oven temperature to 350°F and bake for 30 more minutes. Cool on a wire rack or windowsill until the pie is firm, about 45 minutes. Store any leftovers in a sealed cake safe. The pie will keep for about 5 days.

## PECAN PIE

**Makes one 9-inch pie**

*This is one of my husband's and my favorite pies, so we make this a lot. I usually buy the pecans at the bulk-food store if I can. Some people leave their pecans whole, but I prefer mine chopped up, and so does Joe. I think it tastes better to have the pecans in smaller bites. Pecan is a very rich pie, so you can't have too much at once. I do know some people who will use walnuts, and they call it a poor man's pecan pie. I tried it once with walnuts and it was true, it was hard to tell the difference.*

1 disk My Homemade Pie Dough (page 3) or Pat-a-Pan Piecrust (page 4)
3 large eggs
¼ teaspoon salt
1 cup sugar
¾ cup light corn syrup
2 teaspoons margarine, melted
¾ cup pecans, chopped

Preheat the oven to 350°F.

**For the homemade pie dough crust:** Roll the disk of pie dough out to a ⅛-inch thickness on a floured surface. Fit the dough into a 9-inch pie pan. Trim the overhang to 1 inch. Fold the dough under and crimp the edges.

**For the pat-a-pan piecrust:** Pat the dough with your fingers, first at the sides of the 9-inch pie pan and then across the bottom. Flute the edges.

In a large bowl, beat the eggs well. Add the salt, sugar, corn syrup, and margarine. Place the pecans in the unbaked pie shell. Pour the mixture over the pecans and bake until golden brown, about 1 hour. Cool on a wire rack or windowsill until the pie is firm, about 45 minutes. Store any leftovers in a sealed cake safe. The pie will keep for about 7 days.

## ZUCCHINI PIE

**Makes one 9-inch pie**

*This is an easy recipe that our teacher gave us for cooking class. It will be fun to make this during the summer when Mom has plenty of zucchinis ripening in our garden.*

2 disks My Homemade Pie Dough (page 3)

3 cups peeled, shredded zucchini

1½ teaspoons ground cinnamon

1 tablespoon fresh lemon juice

½ teaspoon ground allspice

1¼ cups sugar

¼ cup all-purpose flour

1 tablespoon butter

Pinch of salt

Preheat the oven to 375°F.

**For the homemade pie dough crust:** Roll both disks of pie dough out to a ⅛-inch thickness on a floured surface. Fit one of the dough disks into a 9-inch pie pan. Trim the overhang to be even with the top of the pie pan. Set the other rolled-out disk of dough aside.

In a large bowl, combine the zucchini, cinnamon, lemon juice, and allspice. Stir until the zucchini is evenly coated, and then add the sugar, flour, butter, and salt. Continue to stir until the mixture is well blended. Spoon into the prepared piecrust. Use some water to wet the rim of the bottom crust, which will help both crusts adhere together. Cover the pie with the top crust, crimping the crusts together all the way around. Bake for 30 to 45 minutes or until golden brown. Cool on a wire rack or windowsill until the pie is firm, about 45 minutes. Store any leftovers in a sealed cake safe. The pie will keep for about 2 days.

### CHILDREN'S BAKING
**Verena, Age 11**

*I started my first cooking class in fourth grade at school. I had been baking cakes at home, so I already know about the different measuring cups and spoons. I like baking and think it is fun to sample what we have made at school. I thought it was funny when a boy in my class asked where the ruler was to start measuring things. I'm always glad when Mom has warm cookies right out of the oven when we get home from school. I like cookies with milk. In the cooking class we learned to make piecrusts. We made pumpkin pie, apple pie, and zucchini pie. We also made chocolate chip cookies and peanut butter cookies. Everyone in my class that is a beginner has a partner from an older grade to help. One day my partner and I went outside to get snow for homemade ice cream. This class makes going to school so much more fun and interesting.*

## MEAT PIES

Pie doesn't have to always be filled with fruits or vegetables. There are many meat pies that make filling and easy meals. Piecrusts can be filled with chicken, pork, or beef to make a delicious dinner.

## BAKED CHICKEN PIE
### Makes two 9-inch pies

*We raise our own carrots, onions, potatoes, peas, and chickens. So we have everything in this recipe on hand, which makes this an easy supper.*

4 disks My Homemade Pie Dough (page 3)
2 cups peeled and diced potatoes
1¾ cups sliced carrots
⅔ cup chopped onion
1 cup (2 sticks) butter, softened
1 cup all-purpose flour
1¾ teaspoons salt

¾ teaspoon ground pepper
2 tablespoons chicken soup base
3 cups chicken broth
1½ cups milk
4 cups cubed cooked chicken
1 cup fresh or frozen peas

Preheat the oven to 425°F.

*For the homemade pie dough crust:* Roll 2 disks of pie dough out to a ⅛-inch thickness on a floured surface. Fit each of the dough disks into a 9-inch pie pan. Trim the overhang to be even with the top of the pie pan. Set the other 2 rolled-out dough disk aside.

Boil the potatoes and carrots in a large saucepan over medium heat until almost tender, about 10 minutes. Drain and set aside. In a large skillet, sauté the onion and butter until tender. Stir in the flour, salt, pepper, and chicken soup base until blended. Gradually stir in the broth and milk. Cook, stirring, for 2 minutes or until thick. Add the chicken, peas, potatoes, and carrots to the broth mixture. Remove from the heat.

Divide the chicken mixture evenly between the 2 unbaked pie shells. Use some water to wet the rim of the bottom crusts, which will help both crusts adhere together. Cover the pies with the top crusts, crimping the crusts together all the way around. Bake the pies for 35 to 40 minutes, until the crust is golden brown. Cool on a wire rack or windowsill until the pie is firm, about 45 minutes. Store any leftovers covered in a refrigerator or cool cellar. The pie will keep for about 7 days in the refrigerator.

## SHOOFLY PIE

There are many baked goods that the Amish are credited with concocting or co-opting: elephants ears, funnel cakes, and Soft Pretzels (see page 78), to name a few. But perhaps the baked good with the single most Amish identity is shoofly pie. Long before Dinah Shore immortalized the molasses morass in her famous song, the Amish were enjoying this pie. The origins of this pie's unusual name have been debated by food historians for the better part of a century. The most commonly offered explanation is that the name comes from the flies that are attracted to the pools of molasses that sometimes form on top of the pie while it is cooling. Many Amish homemakers set hot pies on a windowsill to catch a cooling breeze in the summer, hence the need to shoo the flies.

Other food historians point to the possibility that the name of the pie is simply an inaccurately translated version of a German or Swiss word. Interestingly, Elizabeth Coblentz, in her first mention of the pie in her column, spelled it "Choo Fly Pie." Whether this was simply an error or a phonetic clue to the recipe's origin went with her when she passed away.

"Shoo Fly Pie and Apple Pan Dowdy
Makes your eyes light up
Your tummy say 'Howdy.'
Shoo Fly Pie and Apple Pan Dowdy
I never get enough of that wonderful stuff."

—DINAH SHORE, "Shoo Fly Pie and Apple Pan Dowdy," 1946

## SHOOFLY PIE

Makes one 9-inch pie

1 disk My Homemade Pie Dough (page 3) or Pat-a-Pan Piecrust (page 4)
1 cup molasses
⅔ cup boiling water
1 teaspoon baking soda

TOPPING:
3½ cups all-purpose flour
1 cup sugar
¾ cup shortening, softened
Dash of salt

Preheat the oven to 350°F.

*For the homemade pie dough crust:* Roll the disk of pie dough out to a ⅛-inch thickness on a floured surface. Fit the dough into a 9-inch pie pan. Trim the overhang to 1 inch. Fold the dough under and crimp the edges.

*For the pat-a-pan piecrust:* Pat the dough with your fingers, first at the sides of the 9-inch pie pan and then across the bottom. Flute the edges.

In a large bowl, combine the molasses, boiling water, and baking soda. Pour the mixture into the unbaked pie shell.

*To make the topping:* In a large bowl, mix the flour with the sugar, shortening, and salt. Spread this on top of the molasses mixture in the pie shell. Bake until the center of the pie is set, about 45 minutes. Cool on a wire rack or windowsill until the pie is firm, about 45 minutes. Store any leftovers in a sealed cake safe. The pie will keep for about 5 days.

# BREADS · ROLLS · PASTRIES

## Chapter Two

*"While often sliced and served for supper, fresh bread can be found on the table at any meal of the day.*
*I used to make a lot more bread when all of our children were still living at home—usually about nine loaves a week.*
*I would bake the bread before they came so when they got in the door it was good and warm."*

— ELIZABETH COBLENTZ, 1998

Among the Amish, bread is a symbol of self-sustainability and sustenance. The ability to transform grain into flour and then into baked bread is a cornerstone of the Amish kitchen. And despite their culture being under assault by our nation of fast food, fast cars, and nutritional waste, most Amish homemakers can be found at some point throughout the week with their hands wrist deep in dough, kneading as generations before taught them. One of my first glimpses inside the kitchen of an Amish homemaker was of a teenage Amish girl not much older than me at the time, kneading the dough for a loaf of bread under the watchful eye of her mother, who once did the same under the watchful eye of her mother.

Our society, which has transformed hand-made softness into factory-produced blandness, seems to have little use for bread beyond sandwiches. But the Amish will use their homemade breads in stuffings, soups, French toast, puddings, and pies. Whether it's white, wheat, sourdough, or salt-rising, homemade bread is a value and a virtue passed down through generations of Amish cooks.

Some Amish will buy store-bought bread, but one group that will not is the Swartzentruber sect. This is the most conservative branch of the Amish religion. Church members are not permitted to work outside the homestead. Men make their living through farming or

through other home-based businesses that don't need to interconnect with the "outside world." I once stopped at the home of a Swartzentruber and saw winter wheat neatly stacked in the surrounding fields. The wheat, I'm sure, would be used to bake bread. The home had not a single bow to modernity, like indoor plumbing or gas appliances, that some other Amish homes have. The Swartzentrubers are the last of the purely agrarian and insular Amish. An Amish homemaker from the conservative Swartzentruber sect would never be seen in a supermarket; they obtain virtually all of their sustenance from the earth, feasting or famishing with the harvest tides.

For a number of years in the Amish community of Berne, Indiana, there were two grocery stores. One was a sparkling-clean, more modern supermarket with electronic scanners and an in-store bakery. The other grocery store, one that looked like it had seen better days, a rather sleepy-looking affair, managed to hold on well into the 1990s with its manual cash registers and dim lights. Several area Amish bishops would only allow their congregations to shop at the sleepy-looking grocery because they were not allowed to use the electronic scanners found in the other store. Change comes slowly to the Amish, but this prohibition was dropped at some point in the 1990s and the tired-looking store promptly closed, as the Amish preferred the bigger and brighter store.

## BAKING BREAD WITH LOVINA

I always enjoyed the days when I was a young girl coming home from school. I'd find my mother taking freshly baked bread out of the oven. The warm, moist slices spread with melting butter were a very good treat for us hungry children. Sometimes we'd spread apple butter on the bread too. This was the apple butter that we had helped Uncle Chris make in his big black kettle over the open fire. I now know the feeling when my children come home from school and see the bread still warm from baking. They always enjoy a few slices of bread spread with butter and jam.

There are many different kinds of breads. At our church services, homemade wheat and white breads are always served. Usually around twenty loaves of each are baked. We women folks help each other bake bread for each other's services. I remember the first time I baked white bread shortly after we were married. It seemed to work out really well for me, and I felt proud to take out the nice loaves of bread from the oven. I took several loaves to our annual Christmas gathering at my parents' house that year. Everyone seemed to really like it, which gave me the encouragement to keep trying.

Now it seems I do a lot more sourdough bread. A loaf of homemade sourdough bread will stay fresh for over a week, which is longer than other kinds. Regular yeast bread seems to dry out more quickly, and sourdough is more of a moist bread. I make both kinds, but if I have a choice I prefer the Homemade Bread (page 49), especially for sandwiches. My four oldest daughters have mixed together the sourdough bread. It is a lot easier to work with than the basic white bread. And it doesn't take any yeast either, since you do it with a starter. At times I do like changing off from the sourdough bread to another kind.

When stirring up bread dough, I have noticed that if one of the girls does it, she sometimes don't mix it well enough. Yet adding the flour too fast can make it less smooth and the bread won't be as soft. I always put in all the liquid ingredients first and the flour always last. And then I always like to rub some olive oil or vegetable oil on the top and bottom of the dough before I let it rise. It seems like this softens up the dough so I don't have that hard crust on top when it is rising. On the other hand, if you let the loaf rise too high, the loaf won't be as moist. Once you put the dough in the oven it will kind of rise while it is baking. Freshly baked bread is okay to slice while still warm, but it is better to leave it overnight before slicing. We all like warm bread, but the bread slices and tastes better the next day. You can always stick bread in your oven for a few minutes to warm it up before serving.

Toast from homemade bread is also a favorite around here in the mornings, but, of course, we don't have one of those electric toasters. So I usually use my broiler on the bottom of my oven to make toast. Or sometimes I will just butter each side and put it in a pan and toast it on my gas stove. You have to flip the toast to brown each side whether you are using a broiler or a stove-top pan. When I was growing up at home we had a kerosene stove and would just put the toast on top of the burner.

## HOMEMADE BREAD

### Makes 1 loaf

*When Mom would make large batches of bread, she would use a bread dough mixer. Her bread dough mixer consists of a stainless steel bucket with a handle that curves, and you turn a knob on top and stir. She would use it if she had to make three or four batches of bread at one time. I've tried using hers, but I prefer to knead mine by hand.*

*An unusual thing that Mom would do with bread—and I think this is just an older custom—is to bake multiple loaves in the same pan. She would put three loaves of bread in a 9 by 13-inch cake pan because she didn't have enough loaf pans. The piece of bread where the loaves met would always be the best because there was no crust. Somehow she made sure the loaves didn't overlap.*

*I've tried many recipes for homemade white bread through the years, but I keep coming back to this one, which is what my mother used. Her recipe calls for lard, but the recipe also works well with vegetable shortening.*

1 package active dry yeast
2½ cups lukewarm water
Lard (amount the size of an egg)
2 tablespoons sugar
1 tablespoon salt
Enough bread flour to make a soft dough

Grease a 5 by 9-inch loaf pan and set aside.

In a small bowl, dissolve the yeast in ½ cup of the warm water. In a large bowl, combine the lard, sugar, salt, and the remaining 2 cups of water. Add the yeast mixture to the bowl and stir until combined. Add the flour, ½ cup at a time, mixing until the dough is elastic and doesn't stick to the sides of the bowl. Cover the bowl loosely with plastic wrap or a damp cloth and let rise until double in size, about 1½ hours in a warm, draft-free place.

Punch the dough down and form it into a loaf with your hands. Place the dough into the prepared loaf pan. Cover with a damp cloth and let rise again until the dough is level with the loaf pan, about an hour.

While the dough is rising, preheat the oven to 325°F.

Bake the bread for about 45 minutes. The bread will sound hollow when tapped. After removing the bread from the oven, brush with the butter or margarine for a softer crust. Remove the bread from the pan and cool on a wire rack or windowsill. After the bread cools completely, it can be stored in a sealed plastic bag and frozen where it will keep up to 6 months. If the bread is stored in a sealed plastic bag at room temperature, it should be consumed within 4 days.

## DILLY BREAD
### Makes 12 rolls or 1 loaf

*This is a delicious, moist bread. The dill flavor makes a nice addition to a sandwich. This recipe can also be made into dinner rolls, and the little flakes of dill add a pretty green color to the rolls. Dill can be grown in the garden. Mom's dill would come up year after year, but I haven't had as much luck with mine.*

| | |
|---|---|
| 1 package active dry yeast | 1 cup small-curd cottage cheese |
| ¼ cup warm water | 1 tablespoon dry dill seed or dill weed |
| 2 tablespoons sugar | ¼ teaspoon baking soda |
| 1 tablespoon dried onion flakes | 1 large egg |
| 1 tablespoon butter, softened | 2½ cups bread flour |
| 1 teaspoon salt | |

Dissolve the yeast in the water in a large bowl. Add the sugar, onion flakes, butter, salt, cottage cheese, dill, baking soda, and egg. Mix well. Slowly add the flour, beating after each addition. After all the flour is added and stirred in, you may need to knead the dough with your hands to finish mixing the flour in. Cover with a damp cloth. Let rise in a warm place for 1 hour.

Punch down and shape into 12 rolls or 1 loaf. Grease a baking sheet for the rolls or grease and flour a 5 by 9-inch loaf pan for the loaf. Place the dough on the sheet or in the pan, cover with a damp cloth, and let rise again until light, 30 to 45 minutes.

While the dough is rising, preheat the oven to 350°F. Bake until golden brown, 14 to 16 minutes for the rolls or about 45 minutes for the loaf. Remove the pans from the oven and brush the bread or rolls with melted lard or margarine. Unused rolls or bread can be sealed and frozen, or stored in a sealed container and stay fresh for 3 to 4 days.

## CHILDREN'S BAKING
### Loretta, 8

*I like to help my mom and my sisters make cakes, cookies, and breads. I have the most fun when I can mix up the bread and cookies with my hands. I like to squish the dough between my fingers. I like to help make little balls for cookies. What I like the most is when they are ready to eat. I like to eat the bread when it is still warm and spread butter on it.*

## HOBO BREAD

**Makes 1 small loaf**

*This is a bread full of raisins. Raisins were popular in my household when I was a child since my father really liked them, but I didn't care for them. I do remember that in church when I was a little girl they'd pass around cookies with raisins, and I would take the cookie and pick out the raisins and eat the cookie. But I like them better now as an adult. This recipe calls for soaking the raisins in water overnight, which helps plump them up and soften them in the bread.*

2 cups raisins

4 teaspoons baking soda

1 cup boiling water

4 tablespoons vegetable oil

4 cups all-purpose flour

2 cups sugar

1 cup packed brown sugar

½ teaspoon salt

Mix the raisins, baking soda, and boiling water. Cover and let stand until cooled, or overnight.

Preheat the oven to 350°F. Lightly grease a 4 by 8-inch loaf pan. In a medium bowl, mix the raisin mixture with the oil, flour, sugars and salt. Mix well. Pour into the prepared pan and bake until brown, about 1 hour.

"Of all the housewife duties,
I think it must be said,
There's nothing I like better than
baking homemade bread"

—Poem Posted in an Amish Bakery

## CHEESY BREAD
### Serves 10 to 12

*This is nice, soft bread that is fun for us to eat as a family. We break off pieces and share it among all of us. This tastes best when it is warm right out of the oven. Our family can go through a whole loaf of this in a single sitting!*

| | |
|---|---|
| 1 cup cornmeal | 3 tablespoons sugar |
| 1 teaspoon salt | 3 cups milk |
| ½ teaspoon dry mustard | 1 cup grated Cheddar cheese |
| ¼ teaspoon ground pepper | 6 large eggs |

Preheat the oven to 350°F. Grease a 2-quart casserole and set aside.

Combine the cornmeal, salt, dry mustard, pepper, and sugar in a large saucepan over low heat. When the mixture begins to bubble and thicken, gradually stir in the milk. Continue to cook over low heat and stir constantly until thickened. Stir in the cheese until melted, and remove from the heat. In a separate small bowl, beat the eggs vigorously and stir a small amount (2 to 3 tablespoons) of the hot mixture into the eggs. Then add the eggs to the hot mixture, mixing thoroughly. Pour into the prepared casserole. Bake until puffy and browned, about 45 minutes. Remove the bread from the pan and cool on a wire rack or windowsill. The bread can be stored in a sealed plastic bag and remain fresh for 3 to 4 days. This bread does not freeze well.

## AMISH ESTATE AUCTIONS

The Amish are not a materialistic people. Their culture de-emphasizes clutter and material goods. This is not to say that the Amish are not sentimental, though. Quite the opposite is true. Amish sentimentality is infused in intangibles: *memories* and *stories*. Possessions are often viewed simply as empty vessels that have no role to play in the better life beyond. This cultural view of possessions makes up the underpinnings of the "estate auction." Often after a death, the deceased's possessions are auctioned off. Everything. If a loved one wants an item badly enough, he or she will bid for it at the auction. Such sentimental items might be a sewing machine, a special dish, or a quilt. With most Amish families being quite large, the auction also underscores another cornerstone of the culture: egalitarianism. Nasty estate fights that sully the world of non-Amish postmortems are far less frequent among the plain people. Monies raised at the auction are divided among siblings equally, and that's the end of it. With so many people attending an auction and competing for items, sometimes items can just slip away.

The estate auction for Lovina's mother, Elizabeth Coblentz, was quite typical. Most in attendance were Amish. A handful of "Amish Cook" column fans showed up, which probably skewed bids a little higher than in a typical auction. After the auction, the affairs of the deceased are wrapped up, and all that is left are memories.

## SALT-RISING BREAD

### Makes 3 medium loaves

*I like to try different breads. This one uses salt instead of yeast to rise, so it is a good one for people who can't eat yeast. Mom ran this recipe in her column back in the 1990s.*

1½ tablespoons salt

2 tablespoons cornmeal

2½ cups sliced potatoes

1 quart boiling water

1 teaspoon baking soda

1½ teaspoons sugar

11 cups all-purpose flour

1 cup milk

1 tablespoon shortening, melted

In a large bowl, sprinkle 1 tablespoon of the salt and the cornmeal over the potatoes. Add the boiling water and stir until the salt has dissolved. Cover and keep in a warm place, like a sunny window, for 20 hours.

Drain off the liquid into a separate large bowl. Add the baking soda, sugar, and 5 cups of the flour to the liquid. Stir until the ingredients are well blended. This sponge should be the consistency of cake batter. Set the mixture in a warm place, and let rise until light and full of bubbles, about 1½ hours.

In a heavy saucepan over medium-high heat, scald the milk and cool to lukewarm. Add the shortening and stir to combine. Add the milk mixture and the remaining 6 cups of flour to the sponge. Mix until an elastic dough forms. Knead for 10 to 12 minutes on a lightly floured surface, and then divide into 3 loaves. Let rise in a warm place until light in texture, about 1½ hours.

While the dough is rising, preheat the oven to 350°F. Grease and flour three 5 by 9-inch loaf pans.

Put the dough into the prepared pans and bake until golden brown, 1 hour.

Remove the bread from the pan and cool on a wire rack or windowsill. After the bread cools completely, it can be stored in a sealed plastic bag and frozen where it will keep up to 6 months. If the bread is stored in a sealed plastic bag at room temperature, it should be consumed within 4 days.

## DOUBLE-CINNAMON BREAD

Makes 1 loaf

*I have a habit when I make something with cinnamon of putting in twice as much as the recipe calls for because I like the taste so much. This cinnamon bread would be great as cinnamon toast!*

2 cups milk

2 tablespoons active dry yeast

½ cup warm water

1 cup sugar

2 teaspoons salt

½ cup shortening, softened

2 large eggs, beaten

2 tablespoons ground cinnamon

7 to 8 cups bread flour

FILLING:

½ cup (1 stick) butter, melted

¼ cup sugar

2 tablespoons ground cinnamon

In a small saucepan, scald the milk over low heat. Remove from the heat and set aside to cool. Dissolve the yeast in the warm water and let sit until bubbles form, about 10 minutes. In a large bowl, mix the milk, yeast mixture, sugar, salt, shortening, eggs, cinnamon, and flour until you get a smooth, elastic dough. Put the bowl in a warm place and allow to rise uncovered for 10 minutes. Knead. Let rise loosely covered in a warm place until double in size, about 1 hour.

Punch the dough down and let rise again, this time for about 30 minutes.

On a lightly floured surface, roll the dough out, spread it with the melted butter, and sprinkle it with the sugar and cinnamon. Roll up and put into a 5 by 9-inch loaf pan. Let rise for 30 minutes.

While the dough is rising, preheat the oven to 350°F.

Bake the bread until golden, 30 to 35 minutes. Remove the bread from the pan and cool on a wire rack or windowsill. After the bread cools completely, it can be stored in a sealed plastic bag and frozen where it will keep up to 6 months. If the bread is stored in a sealed plastic bag at room temperature, it should be consumed within 4 days.

## ROLLING PIN MEMORIES

In the winter of 2009, someone contacted my editor and told him about an item of my mother's that this person wanted to return. The stranger had bought it at my mother's estate auction. I was so thrilled to get this back. Mother had several rolling pins, but her main one was like a solid chunk of wood that had been carved. The handles wouldn't turn. Mother got the rolling pin as a gift and had it for years, before I started rolling out dough. I know she was really proud of it when she got it. It was heavier and had a little more power to roll out the dough than the smaller ones.

Some have the marble rolling pins, which are fancier ones, but when I've used them I just couldn't get used to it. My Aunt Lizzie was rolling out pie dough with a marble rolling pin and she told me I needed to get a rolling pin like it. She thought the heavy marble rolled better, but I didn't think so.

### "BYORP!"

Another thing about rolling pins is that if you are a cook and you have to go a day or two before a wedding to help bake pies, they expect you to "bring your own rolling pin." Someone couldn't possibly gather the thirty or forty rolling pins needed, so everyone needs to come prepared. The first time I was a cook in this way, it was at my cousin's wedding and I had been married for a couple of years, and Mother said, "Don't forget your rolling pin."

I was glad she reminded me because this was my first time being a cook at someone else's wedding.

I was able to get some kitchen items at Mother's auction, including some of her stainless steel kettles and her roasters that I can bake in. I also have her bread mixer. She had so many utensils because they didn't have a wedding wagon when my sisters and I were married. Wedding wagons are "mobile kitchens" equipped with everything needed to prepare large amounts of food (see page 195). Without a wedding wagon, Mom had to furnish everything to cook the wedding meal. I can already see that with having the church dishes in the wedding wagons around here, I won't need as much as Mother did when my daughters are getting married someday.

## The Amish Cook's Bread Tips

- *Lukewarm or warm water should be around 100°F.*

- *For yeast sold in bulk-food stores, 1 tablespoon of loose yeast equals about one package of yeast.*

- *Yeast can be frozen for long-term keeping.*

- *Dry active yeast needs to be soaked in the warm water for 10 to 15 minutes before adding it in any recipe. Instant yeast can be added directly in a recipe.*

- *Remove bread from pans upon removing them from the oven and cool on racks to keep the bread from getting soggy.*

## PINEAPPLE BREAD

### Makes 1 loaf

*This bread is a bit lighter than denser zucchini or pumpkin breads. This tastes great with cream cheese on top.*

2 cups all-purpose flour

2 teaspoons baking powder

¼ teaspoon baking soda

¾ cup packed brown sugar

3 tablespoons butter, softened

2 large eggs

1 (8-oz) can crushed pineapple, undrained

2 teaspoons ground cinnamon

2 teaspoons sugar

Preheat the oven to 350°F. Grease a 5 by 9-inch loaf pan and set aside.

In a bowl, whisk together the flour, baking powder, and baking soda. In a large bowl, combine the brown sugar, butter, and eggs, and stir well; then mix in the pineapple and its juices. Gradually begin adding the flour mixture to the pineapple mixture, and stir until thoroughly combined. Pour the batter into the prepared loaf pan, and sprinkle the top with the cinnamon and sugar. Bake for 40 minutes, or until a toothpick inserted in the center of the bread comes out clean. Cool the bread on a wire rack for 15 minutes, then remove from the pan and cover with plastic wrap until ready to serve. Remove the bread from the pan and cool on a wire rack or windowsill. The bread can be stored in a sealed plastic bag and remain fresh for 3 to 4 days. This bread does not freeze well.

## BANANA NUT BREAD
### Makes 1 loaf

*I don't care for bananas when they are mushy, but in a bread they taste really good. It seems our whole family likes bananas. I can remember one night when we were in a grocery store and we had four-year-old Kevin along, and he saw some bananas. I wasn't planning to buy any that night, but he just really wanted them, so I bought a bunch. As soon as we got home, he started eating them up. My mom would wait for the bananas to get as ripe as they could before eating them, but for me, as soon as they turn brown I don't like them. If I didn't get them over to Mom's, I would use them up in bread.*

1 cup sugar

2 tablespoons margarine

1 large egg

3 teaspoons thick sour milk

1 teaspoon baking soda

2 cups all-purpose flour

½ cup walnut pieces

1 cup mashed very ripe bananas

Preheat the oven to 350°F. Lightly grease a 5 by 9-inch loaf pan and set aside.

In a large bowl, combine the sugar, margarine, egg, milk, and baking soda. Then sift in the flour, and add the walnuts and bananas. Mix very well. Pour into the prepared pan and bake for 1 hour. A butter knife inserted into the center of the bread will come out clean when the bread is done.

Remove the bread from the pan and cool on a wire rack or windowsill. The bread can be stored in a sealed plastic bag and remain fresh for 3 to 4 days. This bread does not freeze well.

**BAKING TIP:**
To make sour milk: Put 1 tablespoon lemon juice or vinegar in a measuring cup. Fill with whole milk to make 1 cup. Let sit at room temperature for 15 minutes. The milk should become thick and lumpy.

## A VISIT TO A BULK-FOOD STORE

Bulk-food stores are repositories of large amounts of flours, cake mixes, sugars, and spices. Most Amish communities have at least one bulk store, but the stores increasingly find themselves serving two bases of clientele: Amish and non-Amish.

Non-Amish customers come seeking chocolate-covered pretzels, snack mixes, and spices perhaps not found at a typical supermarket.

Amish customers come as they always have, for reasons that haven't changed: Large families have a large need for staples. At the Miller Bulk Food store in Adams County, Ohio, one might not see the largest sacks of staples on the shelves, but they're ready for the Amish coming in who seek them.

"We have flour and sugar in fifty-pound bags in the back. They know we have them and they'll come in and buy them when needed," says Leah Miller, the store's proprietor.

The shelves are full of many typically hard-to-find mixes, like gingerbread or spice cake mix, for either the busy Amish baker or the "English" customer seeking something unique.

A scan of Miller's shelves shows clear bags of pecan pie base, gingerbread cake mix, angel food cake mix, and meringue powder. Other less traditionally Amish offerings like curry powder and wasabi trail mix add to the variety. Premade pie fillings and vats of honey also beckon the busy baker.

At Fountain Acres Bulk Foods and Bakery, over 100 miles away in Indiana, the selection of goods is equally impressive. Sugar, flour, and cornmeal are available there as well in 50-pound sacks. Bulk bags of homemade noodles and potpie soup line whole shelves for the Pennsylvania Dutch. A huge selection of bagged oatmeal beckons the oat aficionado. Bulk bags of apple bars, strawberry bars, hot chocolate

mix, and chocolate milk mix compete for space with more offbeat items like chai tea and gummy worms, not typically thought of as Amish fare. On a busy Saturday, customers—Amish and English—load up their carts with bulk items. Gaslights hiss above, adding ambiance and light to the store.

## SWEET BREAKFAST ROLLS

**Makes 2 dozen rolls**

*We don't often have sweets in the morning, but when we do this recipe is a good one to make. Our children like their sweet snacks in the afternoon when they come home from school. Joe likes a cinnamon roll or sweet roll in the morning with his hot chocolate or coffee.*

1 cup milk, scalded

½ cup (1 stick) butter

2 teaspoons salt

½ cup sugar

2 packages active dry yeast

½ cup warm water

4 large eggs, beaten

6 cups bread flour

4 tablespoons (½ stick) butter, softened

½ cup sugar

1 tablespoon ground cinnamon

Grease a jelly-roll pan or a large cookie sheet with a 1-inch rim.

In a large bowl, mix the milk, butter, salt, and sugar. Set the bowl aside until the mixture cools to lukewarm. While the mixture is cooling, dissolve the yeast in the warm water for about 10 minutes or until bubbles form. Then add the yeast mixture, eggs, and flour gradually to the lukewarm milk mixture. Knead with your hands until an elastic dough forms. Remove the dough from the bowl and place on a lightly floured surface. Knead the dough for 5 or 6 strokes, and then roll into a 12 by 20-inch rectangle.

In a small bowl, mix the butter, sugar, and cinnamon until well blended. Spread the mixture over the dough. Roll the dough up from the 20-inch side. Cut the 20-inch-long roll into ¾-inch pieces and place on the prepared pan. Let the dough rise uncovered for about 30 minutes.

While the dough is rising, preheat the oven to 350°F. Bake the rolls until golden brown, 20 minutes. Add frosting (see Basic Frosting, page 119).

## RAISIN BREAD

**Makes 2 loaves**

*My father liked raisins and prunes. This bread has a lot of raisins and a thick texture from the mashed potatoes. Try this warm and spread with butter for a great breakfast! The raisins will have much more flavor if chopped before being added to the dough.*

1½ cups milk

¼ cup sugar

2 teaspoons salt

½ cup (1 stick) butter, softened

1 cup unseasoned mashed potatoes

2 packages active dry yeast

½ cup warm water

1½ cups raisins

7½ cups bread flour

**FILLING:**

½ cup sugar

2 teaspoons ground cinnamon

½ cup (1 stick) butter, softened

In a heavy saucepan, scald the milk over medium heat. Remove from the heat just before the milk reaches the boiling point, then add the sugar, salt, butter, and mashed potatoes and stir. Let cool. In a large bowl, dissolve the yeast in the warm water. Then mix with the milk mixture. Add the raisins and flour. Stir. Let rise in a warm place for 1½ hours, until double in size. Divide the dough into 2 balls.

**To make the filling:** In a separate bowl, mix the filling ingredients until crumbly in texture.

Preheat the oven to 350°F. Grease two 5 by 9-inch loaf pans.

Roll each ball of dough out on a lightly floured surface. Spread half of the filling mixture on the rolled-out dough. Starting with a short side, roll up as for a jelly roll and pinch the edges together at the ends. Place into a loaf pan, making sure all the edges remain sealed. Repeat with the second ball of dough. Place both loaf pans on a baking sheet and bake until golden brown, about 45 minutes. Serve warm.

Remove the bread from the pan and cool on a wire rack or windowsill. After the bread cools completely, it can be stored in a sealed plastic bag and frozen where it will keep up to 6 months. If the bread is stored in a sealed plastic bag at room temperature, it should be consumed within 4 days.

## TOMATO CHEESE BREAD

**Makes 2 loaves**

*Tomatoes are a big hit in our family. We are excited in the summer when we can start using tomatoes in sandwiches, soups, and even bread. My mother would always plant about a hundred tomato plants every year. I don't plant quite that many, but I like to put out at least sixty plants of different varieties. One of my favorites is beefsteak or big beef tomatoes. Also, Early Girl, Big Boy, Roma, and Jetstar are kinds I've tried. My daughter Lovina likes to eat one slice of tomato after another. She would live just on tomatoes if I'd let her. She'll eat them for breakfast, for a snack, or at any meal. I do have a few children who don't care for them, so this bread isn't high on their list. I can make this bread using our own homemade tomato juice, but store-bought is okay to use also.*

2 cups tomato juice

2 tablespoons butter

3 tablespoons sugar

¼ cup ketchup

¼ cup grated Cheddar cheese

1 teaspoon salt

½ teaspoon dried oregano

½ teaspoon dried basil

1 package active dry yeast dissolved in ¼ cup warm water

4 cups all-purpose flour

Grease and lightly flour 2 bread pans. Set aside.

Heat the tomato juice and butter until the butter is melted. Stir in the sugar, ketchup, cheese, salt, oregano, and basil. Let cool until the mixture is lukewarm. Add the yeast and 3 cups of the flour and beat well. Add the remaining 1 cup flour and stir until well combined. Divide the batter between the pans. Cover and let rise in a warm place until double in bulk, about 1 hour.

While the dough is rising, preheat the oven to 325°F. Bake the bread until a toothpick inserted in the center comes out clean, about 35 minutes. The loaves will brown only slightly.

Remove the bread from the pan and cool on a wire rack or windowsill. The bread can be stored in a sealed plastic bag and remain fresh for 3 to 4 days. This bread does not freeze well.

## OVERNIGHT BUTTER DINNER ROLLS

### Makes 24 rolls

*Mom made a lot of dinner rolls. For family meals, Mom would often serve rolls for Sunday noon meals, preparing them the night before. We children would cut the rolls in half, spread them with butter, and then close them again. I think the way Mom would make hers was that she would just take her bread recipe and make the dough into little rolls. But I have several different dinner roll recipes that I like to use, including this one.*

2 packages active dry yeast

1¼ cups very warm water (150°F)

3 large eggs

5 cups bread flour

½ cup sugar

1 cup (2 sticks) melted butter

2 teaspoons salt

Sprinkle both packages of yeast into ¼ cup of the very warm water and stir with a fork. Set aside for 10 minutes, until bubbles form. In a large bowl, beat the eggs and then blend in the yeast mixture. Starting with the flour, add 2½ cups of the flour alternately with the remaining 1 cup of very warm water. Then mix in the sugar, ½ cup of the melted butter, and the salt. Mix until smooth. Beat in the remaining 2½ cups of flour to make a soft dough. Cover with a dish towel, put in a warm, draft-free place, and let rise until double in bulk, 1 to 2 hours.

Punch the dough down with vigor, cover with plastic wrap, and refrigerate overnight.

In the morning, grease 24 muffin-tin cups and set aside. Punch the dough down again and divide in half. On a floured board, roll out each half into a rectangle 8 by 15 inches. Spread with the remaining ½ cup of butter. Starting with the long edge, roll up each piece of dough in jelly-roll fashion. With a very sharp knife, cut each roll into twelve 1-inch slices. Place the slices in the prepared muffin tins, cut side up. Let rise until doubled in bulk, 40 minutes to 1 hour.

While the dough is rising, preheat the oven to 400°F. Bake the rolls until golden brown, 8 to 10 minutes. Immediately brush with the butter and serve. Remove the rolls from the pan and cool on a wire rack or windowsill. The rolls can be stored in a sealed plastic bag and remain fresh for 3 to 4 days. These rolls can also be sealed in a plastic bag and frozen for up to 6 months.

## TOP-NOTCH DINNER ROLLS

**Makes 32 rolls**

*Occasionally the local tourism bureau would ask my mom to allow a tour into her home. She'd serve them homemade dinner rolls and bread. The night before, Mom would have weighing scales on the table and wax paper underneath each roll of dough. She'd measure each roll and each loaf of bread so that they would look and be the same size. I still remember her weighing out one roll at a time.*

1 cup warm water

2 packages active dry yeast

½ cup plus 1 tablespoon sugar

1½ cups hot water

½ cup shortening, softened

2½ teaspoons salt

5 cups bread flour, plus more as needed

In a small bowl, stir together the warm water, yeast, and 1 tablespoon of the sugar and let sit until foamy, 10 to 20 minutes. Then, in a large bowl, mix the hot water, shortening, the remaining ½ cup of sugar, and the salt until the shortening is melted. Cool to lukewarm (100 to 110°F), and then add to the yeast mixture, mixing well. Gradually add the flour, beating well after each addition. Work in just enough more flour to make a soft but not sticky dough. Place in a large greased bowl and turn over once to grease the top of the dough. Cover with a dry dish towel and let rise until double in size, about 1 hour.

Punch down the dough and let it rest for 10 minutes. Divide the dough into 32 rolls and place onto a baking sheet. Let rise until double in size, 45 minutes to 1 hour.

While the dough is rising, preheat the oven to 350°F. Bake until lightly browned, about 25 minutes.

Remove the rolls from the pan and cool on a wire rack or windowsill. The rolls can be stored in a sealed plastic bag and remain fresh for 3 to 4 days. The rolls may also be stored in a plastic bag and frozen for up to 6 months.

## CRANBERRY NUT BREAD

### Makes 1 loaf

*When I think of cranberries, it always makes me think of Thanksgiving. When I was in school, in the second or third grade, we had a Thanksgiving feast. Among the things I remember eating at the feast are cranberry salad and cornbread. That gave me a taste for cranberries, which to me makes this bread delicious!*

2 cups all-purpose flour

1 cup sugar

1½ teaspoons baking powder

½ teaspoon baking soda

1 teaspoon salt

1 large egg, beaten

¾ cup orange juice

1 tablespoon orange zest

1 cup vegetable oil

1 cup chopped cranberries

½ cup chopped nuts of your choice

Preheat the oven to 350°F. Grease a 5 by 9-inch pan and set aside.

Sift together the flour, sugar, baking powder, baking soda, and salt. Mix together thoroughly. In a separate large bowl, combine the egg, orange juice, orange zest, oil, cranberries, and nuts until well blended. Then gradually add in the flour mixture and stir until everything is moistened. Pour into the prepared pan and bake for 45 to 50 minutes, until golden brown.

Remove the bread from the pan and cool on a wire rack or windowsill. The bread can be stored in a sealed plastic bag and remain fresh for 3 to 4 days. This bread does not freeze well.

## STRAWBERRY BREAD

**Serves 6 to 8**

*When I was a child, my first job was picking strawberries. I started when I was in sixth or seventh grade and did it on until I was around sixteen or seventeen. My sisters and I would go pick berries with some other Amish children. We would go pick strawberries in the morning until the sun got too hot, always before lunch. Each of us would have two buckets: One would be to pick for our job, and the other would be for "seconds"—strawberries not good enough to pick and sell but still good enough to take home and eat. We had to fill the 4-quart buckets and take them to the end of the row, and they'd give us a token for each full bucket. We'd then cash in the tokens for our pay. If you were a fast picker, you could earn a lot. We would take home our seconds and make things out of them, or just eat them fresh. We home-canned a lot of them into strawberry pie fillings and strawberry jam.*

2 large eggs

½ cup vegetable oil

1 cup sugar

½ teaspoon vanilla extract

½ teaspoon almond extract

1⅔ cups all-purpose flour

½ teaspoon baking powder

½ teaspoon baking soda

½ teaspoon salt

1½ cups chopped strawberries (fresh or lightly drained frozen)

½ cup chopped nuts of your choice

Preheat the oven to 350°F. Grease a 5 by 9-inch pan and set aside.

In a large bowl, beat the eggs until foamy. Add the oil, sugar, vanilla, and almond extract to the eggs and mix well. In another bowl, sift together the flour, baking powder, baking soda, and salt. Add to the oil mixture and stir until just barely moistened. Add the strawberries and nuts and lightly mix, being careful not to overmix. Pour into the prepared pan and bake until nicely browned and a toothpick inserted in the center comes out clean, 50 minutes to 1 hour. If it begins to brown too quickly, place aluminum foil over the top of the bread. This bread freezes well for long-term storage or will keep 3 or 4 days in a sealed container.

## MAPLE NUT TWIST BREAD

### Serves 6 to 8

*This recipe makes me think of several things. In some areas there are Amish who collect sap from trees to make their own maple syrup. The nuts remind me of our two big English walnut trees in Indiana. Mom would sit under the walnut tree and the children would bring her nuts to crack and eat, or she would save them for baking. I miss the tree now because I have to go out and buy them at the bulk-food store. The maple flavoring in this recipe can also be found at most bulk-food stores. I would have people stop in and want to buy some when we had the tree. Wild walnuts have such a very hard shell. I know one Amish lady who said she'd put them on the driveway so that when the milkman came he'd drive over them and partially crack them, and then she wouldn't have to do so much work.*

1 tablespoon active dry yeast dissolved in ¼ cup warm water

¾ cup milk

4 tablespoons (½ stick) butter, melted

1 large egg

½ teaspoon salt

3 tablespoons granulated sugar

1 teaspoon maple flavoring

3 cups bread flour

FILLING:

4 tablespoons (½ stick) butter, softened

½ cup packed brown sugar

⅓ cup walnuts, chopped

1 teaspoon maple flavoring

1 teaspoon ground cinnamon

Preheat the oven to 350°F. Lightly butter a round 9-inch pizza pan and set aside.

Combine the yeast mixture, milk, and melted butter. Beat in the egg, salt, sugar, and maple flavoring. Gradually stir in the flour. Place in an ungreased bowl and cover with a damp dish cloth. Let rise in a warm place until double in bulk, about 1 hour.

Punch down and divide the dough in half. Press and stretch the first half of the dough into the prepared pan.

**To make the filling:** In a large bowl stir the butter, brown sugar, nuts, maple flavoring, and cinnamon until creamy. Spread the filling over the dough. With buttered hands, stretch the remaining dough large enough to fit over the filling. Place it on top of the filling and lightly press the edges together to seal. Bake until golden brown, 20 minutes. Remove the bread from the pan and cool on a wire rack or windowsill. The bread can be stored in a sealed plastic bag and remain fresh for 3 to 4 days. This bread does not freeze well.

## MYSTERY BISCUITS

**Makes 12 biscuits**

*The mayonnaise and milk give this biscuit a very moist flavor. I think that is why they are so popular among the children in my house.*

2 cups all-purpose flour
1 tablespoon baking powder
1 teaspoon salt
¼ cup mayonnaise
1 cup milk
1 teaspoon sugar

Preheat the oven to 375°F. Grease a baking sheet or 12 muffin cups and set aside.

In a large bowl, combine the flour, baking powder, and salt. Blend in the mayonnaise, milk, and sugar until the mixture is creamy. Drop by the tablespoon onto the prepared pan or fill the muffin cups two-thirds full. Bake until golden brown, 18 to 20 minutes.

### CHILDREN'S BAKING
**Lovina, 4, and Kevin, 3**

*Lovina and Kevin like "mystery biscuits" with sausage gravy for breakfast. They always like pulling the biscuits into little pieces before we add the gravy. If I have leftover biscuits, I set them in a container on the countertop. When they get hungry for a snack they will eat just the plain biscuits. Mystery biscuits are a big hit in our household. They are very easy and simple to make and are moist and have a good flavor.*

## BUTTERMILK BISCUITS
### Makes 12 biscuits

*Buttermilk isn't something I buy very often. But I do substitute sour milk for the buttermilk, and it is almost the same. One cup of thick, sour milk equals 1 cup of buttermilk. Mom never worried about sour milk. She would always say that it's things like spoiled meat that will affect someone, but she never heard of anyone getting sick over sour milk. We'd use milk that was just starting to sour for sour cream and lots of baked goods. I don't think many people would try this recipe if it were called "sour milk biscuits"! These are good with gravy or with butter or jelly.*

2 cups all-purpose flour

¼ cup vegetable oil

¾ teaspoon salt

3 teaspoons baking powder

1 cup (2 sticks) butter, softened

1 cup buttermilk or sour milk

1 teaspoon baking soda

Preheat the oven to 400°F. Lightly grease a baking sheet and set aside.

In a large bowl, combine the flour, vegetable oil, salt, baking powder, butter, milk, and baking soda. Stir with a wooden spoon until the mixture forms a smooth batter. Drop by the teaspoon onto the prepared baking sheet. Bake until golden brown, 10 to 15 minutes.

## AMISH COOK FLASHBACK

Mom had some of her recipes—the ones she made the most—in her head. But she also had written recipes, most of them hand-written. They didn't have as many cookbooks years ago. I don't think Mom liked it when we girls went through her recipe box, because she knew where everything was and we sometimes changed things around.

## DOUBLE-QUICK DINNER ROLLS

### Makes 12 rolls

*As the name implies, this is probably my fastest dinner roll to make. I'll prepare these in a pinch if company suddenly drops in for supper and I want to serve rolls. I like these because they are prepared using muffin tins, which makes them easy to pop into a basket to serve.*

1 package active dry yeast

¾ cup warm water (115°F)

¼ cup sugar

1 teaspoon salt

2¼ cups bread flour

1 large egg

¼ cup shortening or butter (½ stick), softened

Preheat the oven to 350°F.

In a small bowl, dissolve the yeast in the warm water. Let stand for 10 minutes or until bubbles form. In a large bowl, combine the yeast mixture with the sugar, salt, and 1 cup of the flour. Beat thoroughly for 2 minutes. Add the egg and shortening. Then gradually beat in the remaining flour until smooth. Drop the dough into 12 muffin cups. Bake until the tops of the rolls are a nice golden brown, 10 minutes. Remove the bread from the pan and cool on a wire rack or windowsill. The bread can be stored in a sealed plastic bag and remain fresh for 3 to 4 days. These rolls do not freeze well.

## AMISH DOUGNUTS

**Makes 2 dozen doughnuts**

*I always liked homemade doughnuts dipped in milk when I was a child. As I grew older, I would dip them in my coffee. Doughnuts, even if they are a couple of days old, are good dunked in either milk or coffee, which will soften them. I like them best if they have glaze on them.*

½ cup granulated sugar

1 teaspoon salt

6½ cups bread flour

½ cup shortening, softened

3 large eggs, separated

½ cup unseasoned mashed potatoes

2 packages active dry yeast

2 cups milk, scalded and cooled

1 teaspoon ground nutmeg

GLAZE:

3 tablespoons water

1 cup powdered sugar

In a large bowl, sift together the sugar, salt, and flour. Blend the shortening into the dry ingredients.

Combine the egg yolks with the potatoes. Add to the dry ingredients. Add the yeast to the cooled milk. Gradually blend into the flour mixture. Let rise for 40 minutes.

Roll the dough ⅜ inch thick. Cut the dough into 4-inch rounds, a juice glass works great. Repeat until you've used all the dough. Let the doughnuts rise again on a baking sheet, about 45 minutes. Heat lard or vegetable oil in a deep pan to a depth of 2 to 3 inches until very hot. Fry the doughnuts in batches until golden, about 30 seconds on each side.

**To make the glaze:** Mix together the water and sugar. Dip the doughnuts into the mixture.

## HOMEMADE BANANA MUFFINS
### Makes 12 muffins

*My children like bananas sliced with home-canned peaches. A mixture of bananas and peaches tastes delicious served over these muffins.*

2 teaspoons baking powder

1 teaspoon salt

½ teaspoon baking soda

½ teaspoon ground nutmeg

2 cups all-purpose flour

¼ cup vegetable oil

1 large egg, slightly beaten

⅓ cup skim milk

1 cup mashed ripe bananas

½ cup granulated sugar

¼ cup packed brown sugar

Preheat the oven to 375°F. Grease and lightly flour 12 muffin cups or line with paper baking cups.

In a large bowl, stir together the baking powder, salt, baking soda, and nutmeg until evenly blended. Add all the remaining ingredients, mixing only until the dry particles are moistened. Fill the prepared muffin cups ⅔ full and bake until golden brown, 20 to 25 minutes.

## OATMEAL MUFFINS

**Makes 12 muffins**

*I buy my oatmeal in bulk-food stores, because I can get the large amounts that I need to feed our family. This is a good recipe to use up some of the excess oats. This muffin would taste good even using other things besides raisins. For example, one could add ½ cup well-drained pineapple, shredded carrots, or chopped apples instead. Nuts could also be added.*

| | |
|---|---|
| 1 cup all-purpose flour | TOPPING: |
| ¼ cup sugar | 2 tablespoons sugar |
| 1 teaspoon ground cinnamon | 2 teaspoons all-purpose flour |
| 1 tablespoon baking powder | 1 teaspoon ground cinnamon |
| ½ teaspoon salt | 1 teaspoon margarine, melted |
| 1 cup quick-cooking rolled oats | |
| ½ cup chopped raisins | |
| 1 large egg, beaten lightly | |
| ¾ cup milk | |
| 1 teaspoon vanilla extract | |
| 3 tablespoons vegetable oil | |

Preheat the oven to 375°F. Grease 12 muffin cups or line with paper baking cups. Set aside.

Sift the flour, sugar, cinnamon, baking powder, and salt into a large bowl. Stir in the oatmeal and raisins. In another bowl, combine the beaten egg, milk, vanilla, and oil. Add this gently to the flour mixture, stirring just until moistened. Spoon the batter into the prepared muffin cups, filling each two-thirds full.

**To make the topping:** Combine the topping ingredients in a small bowl and sprinkle evenly over the muffin batter in the cups. Bake until a toothpick inserted in the muffin centers comes out clean, about 20 minutes. Remove to a wire rack to cool.

## SOFT PRETZELS

Makes 6 medium pretzels

1½ teaspoons active dry yeast

1½ teaspoons sugar

½ teaspoon salt

¾ cup warm water

1¾ cups bread flour

1 large egg

Coarse salt for sprinkling

Preheat the oven to 425°F. Grease a baking sheet.

Mix and dissolve the yeast, sugar, and salt in the warm water. Stir in the flour until a ball forms. Put the dough on a lightly floured surface and knead until smooth. Divide and roll the dough into 6 small ropes and shape into pretzel shapes. Place on the baking sheet. Beat the egg and brush on the unbaked pretzels. Sprinkle with coarse salt. Bake until they are a light golden color, 10 minutes.

# Chapter Three

*"A house should have a cookie jar for when it is half past 3. Children hurry home from school as hungry as can be.*
*There is nothing quite as splendid in filling children up as spicy fluffy ginger cakes and sweet milk in a cup.*
*A house should have a mother waiting with a hug. No matter what a boy brings home a puppy or a bug.*
*For children only loiter when the bell rings to dismiss. If no one is home to greet them with a cookie and a kiss."*

— Author Unknown

While on assignment for a magazine many years ago, I stopped at a tiny Amish-run bakery in northern Indiana. I'm a sucker for a handwritten sign advertising fresh eggs or home-baked bread, and this sign did both. I walked into the tiny bakery and quickly found myself forgetting about the bread. I was captivated by the cookies. There were shelves of neatly bagged chocolate chip, peanut butter, sugar, molasses, and coffee cookies. I selected a bag of buttermilk cookies, an Indiana Amish specialty, covered with a thick pink icing. Even all these years later, I still remember how soft those cookies were and the subtle taste of the buttermilk baked into the cookies.

Snickerdoodles are another cookie with which the Amish are closely identified. I used to buy bags of homemade cinnamon-sprinkled snickerdoodles and chewy oatmeal cookies at the tiny Schwartz Bakery in Indiana. The bakery has since been shuttered, but the cookie memories remain. I, however, don't need a bakery for my Amish cookie fix as an adult. Lovina's daughters bake wonderfully soft cookies that often seem to materialize around the time I visit.

## LOVINA'S COOKIES

It seems like cookies have a hard time staying around in this household. They are just one thing that our family never gets tired of eating. When the girls and I bake cookies, we usually make four or five batches at one time. Making several hundred cookies at once can be a bit time-consuming, but seeing the children's faces light up after coming home from school to fresh-baked cookies makes it well worth the effort. My mother always said that homemade cookies are better for the children than store-bought. Chocolate chip and frosted sugar cookies seem to be favorites in our family. As a child, I would always love to watch my mother as she formed the long loaves for the Overnight Oatmeal Cookies (see page 93). She would form them on a large cutting board, and then she'd put it somewhere to cool overnight. The next morning she would slice off the cookies and put them on baking sheets to bake. It was always a treat to taste the warm cookies right out of the oven. I always let my children sample cookies while I bake them, as I know how I used to look forward to that.

Our children enjoy cookies and milk as a snack, which I—and my husband—also did as children. Sometimes I do have to hide the cookie container, as they do seem to disappear too fast on occasion. My husband, Joe, also enjoys cookies for a snack in his lunch bucket.

My children like chocolate chips in cookies, but they don't care much for the butterscotch chips.

Two to three hundred cookies are usually made for the church meal that we have after every service. Usually three or four different kinds are made. This is another thing the women folk will help each other with doing. Cookies are also passed around during the services to small children who need a snack.

Cookies can be made for weddings, funerals, and almost any occasion.

When storing cookies in a sealed jar, I add a slice of bread to the container, which helps to keep the cookies soft. One time I put chocolate chip and sugar cookies in the same container. When I opened it the next day, the sugar cookies were hard and dried out and the chocolate chip cookies were nice and soft. The sugar cookies worked like a slice of bread: One dried out to soften the other. I learned my lesson then never to mix one kind of cookie with another in the same container.

I will share some of our family's favorite cookie recipes in this chapter. I think the Pinwheel Cookies (page 83) are some of the prettiest cookies, but I'd have a hard time choosing which one in this chapter is the best tasting!

## PINWHEEL COOKIES

### Makes 3 dozen cookies

*This is a pretty cookie with the swirls of chocolate dough contrasting with the lighter colors. Children love to help make these cookies. They can help roll the dough. I always liked watching Mom when she sliced them and laid them on the baking sheet, because I liked to see the different stripes. You don't see pinwheel cookies as much anymore, probably because they take more time to make.*

1 pound butter, softened

½ teaspoon salt

2 cups sugar

6 teaspoons baking powder

6 cups all-purpose flour

¾ cup milk

4 large egg yolks

6 teaspoons unsweetened cocoa powder

2 teaspoons vanilla extract

In a large bowl, stir together the butter, salt, sugar, baking powder, flour, milk, and egg yolks. Stir vigorously with a wooden spoon until the dough is elastic, adding more flour if needed.

Divide the dough in half. Put one dough half in a bowl and add the cocoa. Knead the dough with your hands until the cocoa is thoroughly mixed in and the dough turns a dark color. Put the other dough half in another bowl, add the vanilla, and work it through the dough until mixed, adding more flour if needed to keep the dough elastic.

On two floured surfaces, roll each dough ball into 9 by 12-inch rectangles about ¼ inch thick. Place the white dough on top of the cocoa dough and press together. Then roll tightly lengthwise, like a jelly roll, into a roll 2 inches in diameter. Set in the refrigerator, covered, for several hours or overnight.

When ready to bake, preheat the oven to 350°F. Slice the dough into ½-inch-thick slices and arrange flat on baking sheets. Bake until the cookies are firm, about 20 minutes. Cool the cookies on a wire rack or a plate and then put into sealed containers. These cookies will stay fresh for up to 5 days.

## BAKING TIP:

When rolling out cookie dough, sprinkle the surface with powdered sugar instead of flour. Too much flour can make the dough heavy.

## PEANUT BUTTER COOKIES

### Makes 5 dozen cookies

*My mom used a different peanut butter cookie recipe. However, when I tried this recipe for the first time I furnished a container of them for church. I had so many people ask me for the recipe and received so many compliments that I like this one, too. When baking, I prefer to use creamy peanut butter.*

1 cup shortening, softened
1 cup granulated sugar
1 cup packed brown sugar
2 large eggs
1 teaspoon vanilla extract
1 cup creamy peanut butter
3 cups all-purpose flour
2 teaspoons baking soda
½ teaspoon salt

Preheat the oven to 350°F.

In a large bowl, cream together the shortening, sugars, eggs, and vanilla until thoroughly mixed. (Editor's note: While Amish cooks would not have an electric mixer, one can be used for this recipe on the lowest setting.) Stir in the peanut butter, flour, baking soda, and salt. The batter will be thick and should be stirred vigorously with a wooden spoon or kneaded with your hands in the bowl until everything is thoroughly mixed. Chill the dough for 1 hour.

Remove the dough from the refrigerator. Shape the dough into 1½-inch balls and place 3 inches apart on ungreased baking sheets. Press each cookie with the back of a floured fork to make a crisscross pattern on top. Bake until the edges are brown, 12 to 14 minutes. Remove from the oven and leave on the baking sheet for a few minutes before transferring to a cooling rack and then put into sealed containers. These cookies will stay fresh for up to 5 days.

## OLD-FASHIONED GINGER COOKIES

**Makes 4 dozen cookies**

*I always like to keep ginger on hand for cookies and other recipes that ask for ginger. The flavor of ginger seems to mix well with molasses while baking.*

1 cup shortening, softened

1½ cups molasses

1 cup butter, softened

1 cup sugar

2 cups buttermilk or sour milk

5½ cups all-purpose flour

½ teaspoon salt

1 tablespoon baking soda

¾ teaspoon ground ginger

1 teaspoon ground cinnamon

In a nonstick saucepan, heat the shortening, molasses, butter, and ½ cup of the sugar over medium heat until melted. Add the milk, stir until smooth, and remove from the heat.

In another bowl, mix the flour, salt, baking soda, ginger, and cinnamon together. Stir in the liquid ingredients until a smooth dough forms. The dough may seem too soft, but don't add more flour. Chill the dough in the refrigerator for at least 2 hours.

Preheat the oven to 350°F. Removed the chilled dough from the refrigerator and roll into 2½-inch balls. In a small, shallow bowl, pour the remaining ½ cup sugar. Dip and roll the dough balls into the sugar and place 2½ inches apart on baking sheets. Flatten the dough gently with the back of a spoon. Bake until the centers begin to turn dark brown, 20 to 25 minutes. Cool the cookies on a wire rack or a plate and then put into sealed containers. These cookies will stay fresh for up to 5 days.

## HONEY SPICE COOKIES

### Makes 2 to 3 dozen cookies

*Joe used to put honey in his coffee instead of sugar. My dad used to mix lemon juice and honey together for a cold. We'd heat it and the warm mixture would soothe your throat. When I first got married and I needed a spice I'd have to go buy it, but it seems now I am stocked up on most of them, like the ginger required for this recipe. I probably go through more cinnamon than anything else. This is a cookie for which I almost always have the spices on hand to make it.*

¾ cup (1½ sticks) butter, softened

1 cup packed brown sugar

1 large egg

¼ cup honey

2 cups all-purpose flour

2¼ teaspoons baking soda

½ teaspoon salt

1 teaspoon ground ginger

½ teaspoon ground cinnamon

¼ teaspoon ground cloves

Granulated sugar for rolling

Preheat the oven to 350°F.

Cream the butter, brown sugar, egg, and honey together in a large bowl. In a separate bowl, mix together the flour, baking soda, salt, ginger, cinnamon, and cloves. Add the flour mixture to the wet ingredients, a little at a time, until a stiff dough forms. Shape the dough into 1½-inch balls and roll in sugar to coat. Place the balls on ungreased baking sheets and bake until the cookies are golden brown and cracked on top, 10 to 15 minutes. Cool the cookies on a wire rack or a plate and then put into sealed containers. These cookies will stay fresh for up to 5 days.

### CHILDREN'S BAKING
#### Lovina, 4

*I like brownies and cookies and milk. I help wash dishes, but I can't bake yet. When I get five years old I can help bake a cake and go to school. I can't wait to go to school.*

## THIMBLE COOKIES

### Makes 2 dozen cookies

*If you want to have a cookie that isn't too sweet, this would be a good choice. I use strawberry jam in mine. You could even replace the jam with chocolate chips or candy. These are called "thimble cookies" because Amish women will use a thimble to make the tiny holes in the center for filling with jam, but if you don't have one, the back of a small spoon or your thumb could be used.*

1 cup butter (2 sticks), softened

½ cup sugar

4 large eggs

1 teaspoon vanilla extract

2 cups all-purpose flour

½ cup jam, any flavor of your choice

Preheat the oven to 325°F.

In a large bowl, cream the butter and sugar until well blended. Beat in the eggs and vanilla. Work in the flour until a firm dough forms. If the dough seems too sticky, let it chill for a couple of hours in the refrigerator.

Form the dough into 1-inch balls and place 2 inches apart on ungreased baking sheets. Use a clean thimble to press a hole in each one. Fill the hole with a small amount of jam. Bake until the edges of the cookies are golden brown and the jam begins to bubble, about 25 minutes.

Cool the cookies on a wire rack or a plate and then put into sealed containers. These cookies will stay fresh for up to 5 days.

## MILKING TIME

When we were growing up in Indiana, we always had milking cows, usually up to fourteen or fifteen, though sometimes less. We always had to be out there early milking because the milkman would come before sunrise. The milkman would then take our milk to market, where it was sold. I first started milking when I was around seven years old. At first we'd stay on one side of the cow to learn, and we'd maybe help milk with one hand. We had to get used to being near them, but some cows would kick. Sometimes they would manage to kick a full bucket of milk. Joe and I had a few cows for the first several years of our married life. Elizabeth and Susan would go out to the barn and Joe would squirt milk directly from the cow into their cups. They really enjoyed the warm milk. Joe and I don't have any cows here in Michigan, but we'd like to get some again soon because it is really nice to have your own supply of milk.

## HOMEMADE BUTTERMILK COOKIES

### Makes 4 dozen cookies

*Old-fashioned buttermilk is the milk left over after butter has been churned from cream. Store-bought versions are somewhat different, being a bit thicker than the homemade kind. Amish women have found lots of different ways to use up the buttermilk, such as in cookies, pies, cakes, and biscuits. The thick, slightly sweet milk gives a nice flavor and holds up during the baking process.*

1 cup (2 sticks) butter, softened

2 cups sugar, plus more for sprinkling

3 large eggs

1 teaspoon vanilla extract

2 teaspoons baking soda

2 teaspoons cream of tartar

5 cups all-purpose flour

¾ cup buttermilk

Preheat the oven to 350°F.

Cream together the butter and sugar in a large bowl. Add the eggs, beating well. Then add the vanilla. Mix together the baking soda, cream of tartar, and flour. Add the buttermilk and the dry ingredients alternately to the butter mixture. Chill the dough uncovered for several hours.

Roll out and cut out the cookies using a round glass or cookie cutter and place on ungreased baking sheets. Sprinkle with sugar and bake until golden, about 10 minutes.

Cool the cookies on a wire rack or a plate and then put into sealed containers. These cookies will stay fresh for up to 5 days.

## RANGER COOKIES

### Makes 4 dozen cookies

*This is a really good cookie, although I'm not sure why they are named this way. If you want a crunchier cookie, bake them for 5 minutes longer. My husband, Joe, likes these as a crunchier cookie. You can taste the oatmeal and cereal in them. Personally, I prefer these over a chocolate chip cookie. In some Amish communities these are known as "Ranger Joe" cookies.*

1 cup packed brown sugar

1 cup granulated sugar

1 cup shortening, softened

2 large eggs, beaten

1 tablespoon vanilla extract

½ teaspoon salt

½ teaspoon baking soda

½ teaspoon baking powder

2 cups all-purpose flour

2 cups puffed rice cereal

2 cups quick-cooking rolled oats

Preheat the oven to 400°F.

In a large bowl, cream the sugars and shortening. Add the beaten eggs and vanilla to the sugar mixture. Mix thoroughly.

In a separate bowl, sift together the salt, baking soda, baking powder, and flour. Add to the wet mixture. Stir in the cereal and oats. Roll the dough into walnut-size balls and place 2 inches apart on ungreased baking sheets. Bake until golden brown around the edges, about 10 minutes.

Cool the cookies on a wire rack or a plate and then put into sealed containers. These cookies will stay fresh for up to 5 days.

## OVERNIGHT OATMEAL COOKIES

### Makes 5 dozen cookies

*Some people refer to these as "Gay's Icebox Oatmeal Cookies," but we always just call them "Overnight Cookies." I'm not sure where the name Gay's came from, but it is an old recipe for oatmeal cookies that my mother often made. This cookie is great as a snack, but it also is great for breakfast! Mom could mix them up and then slice and bake them the next morning. She would take her big cutting board out of the cabinet and shape a rectangular loaf so that the cookies would be elongated. Mom would shape the loaf, then put the cookie dough in the cellar overnight and bring the board up in the morning to slice and bake them. They are a harder, crunchier cookie.*

1 cup shortening, softened

1 cup packed brown sugar

1 cup granulated sugar

2 large eggs, beaten

1 teaspoon vanilla extract

1 teaspoon baking soda

1 teaspoon salt

1½ cups all-purpose flour

3 cups quick-cooking rolled oats

½ cup sweetened shredded coconut

½ cup walnut pieces

In a large bowl, cream together the shortening and sugars. Then add the eggs and vanilla and mix.

In a separate bowl, sift together the baking soda, salt, and flour. Combine the dry ingredients with the sugar mixture. Stir in the oatmeal, coconut, and nuts. Mix well.

Divide the dough into thirds. On a lightly floured board or wax paper, roll each third into a log about 2 inches in diameter and 10 to 12 inches long. Refrigerate uncovered for at least 2 hours or overnight.

When ready to bake, preheat the oven to 350°F. Slice the rolled dough logs into pieces about ¾ inch thick and bake on ungreased baking sheets until golden brown, about 14 minutes. Let cool on the pans for 1 to 2 minutes before removing to a cooling rack. Cool the cookies on a wire rack or a plate and then put into sealed containers. These cookies will stay fresh for up to 5 days.

> **BAKING TIP:**
> Some cookie dough works better if chilled for an hour or two before baking. If a cookie dough is too sticky, chilling it for a while can make it easier to handle. Cookie dough that needs to be sliced also benefits from being chilled for 45 minutes to 1 hour before baking.

## SPRITZ COOKIES

**Makes 5 dozen cookies**

*This is an old favorite in some Amish communities. The cookies are small in size, but sweet in flavor. If you don't have a cookie press as the recipe calls for, the batter can be dropped by the teaspoon full onto a baking sheet.*

**1 cup (2 sticks) butter, softened**
**⅔ cup sugar**
**3 large egg yolks**
**1 teaspoon vanilla extract**
**2½ cups all-purpose flour**

Preheat the oven to 400°F.

Mix the butter, sugar, egg yolks, and vanilla together thoroughly in a large bowl. Add the flour and mix well. Using one-quarter of the dough at a time, shape through a cookie press onto ungreased baking sheets. Bake until set but not brown, 7 to 10 minutes. Cool the cookies on a wire rack or a plate and then put into sealed containers. These cookies will stay fresh for up to 5 days.

## BAKING TOOLS

While non-Amish kitchens have morphed into a miasma of electric bread machines, toaster ovens, and food processors, the Amish baker's tools have largely stayed the same.

A young Amish homemaker lists her spatula, rolling pin, and a cookie scoop for putting cookie dough on a baking sheet as her most important items. A hand-cranked egg beater also makes the list.

At Unity Variety, in the tiny town of the same name in Ohio, Amish customers peruse the baking aisle of the store. The proprietor is a kindly woman preparing to sell the store to a younger owner. She walks down the dim gaslit aisle of her store and points to her top seller, a 24 by 24-inch baking sheet that "could easily hold 24 or 25 cookies," she says. Huge stainless steel canners and stockpots also beckon.

There are other, quirkier items that can make life easier for an Amish baker without bowing to modernity. For instance, the Unity store sells an all-in-one apple corer, slicer, and peeler that hooks with a vise onto a countertop. Another slightly more expensive model adheres with suction. Another innovation is the hand-cranked "blender," which can be used to make milkshakes and other confections that typically require an electric counterpart.

At Miller's Dry Goods outside of Richmond, Indiana, proprietor Ada Miller says that her Amish customers seek out a variety of tools for their baking. Her store features a range of handy baking items for the Amish. "Cake pans, bread pans, and tomato presses are some of our top-selling kitchen items," she says. Dippers, spatulas, and plate scrapers are also popular.

For Amish bakers, however, the best is basic.

"For me the most important items are my wooden spoons," says Marianne Miller, an Amish woman in Wayne County.

Lovina's most frequently used tools are wooden spoons, spatulas, measuring cups, and measuring spoons. "I have several sets of the measuring cups and spoons, for when you are doing a lot of baking you don't always have the time to be re-washing," Lovina says.

## BROOMSTICK COOKIES
### Makes 2 dozen cookies

*These cookies resemble broomsticks. They are fun for the children to prepare by rolling the dough between the palms of their hands. You can make the broomsticks different lengths for fun.*

1½ cups shortening

3 cups packed brown sugar

3 large eggs, beaten

1 cup dark corn syrup

¼ cup raisins

2 teaspoons vanilla extract

½ cup walnuts, chopped

6½ to 7 cups all-purpose flour

Powdered sugar or Basic Frosting (page 119)

Preheat the oven to 375°F. Grease baking sheets and set aside.

In a large bowl, cream together the shortening and sugar. Add the beaten eggs and corn syrup and stir.

Put the raisins in a small saucepan and add just enough water to cover. Cook over medium-low heat until all of the water is evaporated, about 10 minutes. Add the cooked raisins, vanilla, and nuts to the shortening mixture. Mix well. Add the flour a little at a time, mixing between each addition, until the mixture resembles pie dough.

Roll pieces of stiff dough between your hands to form thin, 5-inch-long "broomsticks." Place lengthwise on the prepared pans. Bake until golden, about 15 minutes. Let stand for a few minutes before removing from the baking sheets, and then top with powdered sugar or frosting.

Cool the cookies on a wire rack or a plate and then put into sealed containers. These cookies will stay fresh for up to 5 days.

## CHURCH COOKIES
### Makes 10 dozen cookies

*Halfway through the service, cookies, crackers, and pretzels are passed around for the little children. After services, they are passed around for everyone. The reason they call these "Church Cookies" is because they make large amounts. Another reason is because you can make them a week before and they'll still be good. They actually get better if stored in an airtight container in a cool place for a week or so. The days before church are busy enough with preparation, so it is nice to have a cookie that can be done further in advance. This recipe easily halves if you don't need this many cookies. These also make nice holiday cutout cookies.*

3 cups lard

5 cups sugar

5 large eggs

2½ cups milk

3 teaspoons vanilla extract

2 teaspoons baking soda

5 teaspoons baking powder

1 teaspoon salt

11 to 12 cups all-purpose flour, plus more for rolling out

Preheat the oven to 375°F.

In a large bowl, combine the lard and sugar. Add the eggs, beating well. Add the milk and vanilla, and then stir in the dry ingredients until a soft dough forms. Roll the dough out on a lightly floured surface to about a ½-inch thickness. Use cookie cutters to cut into various shapes, or use a glass to make round cookies. Bake until the edges are golden, about 10 minutes.

Cool the cookies on a wire rack or a plate and then put into sealed containers. These cookies will stay fresh for up to 2 weeks.

## WORLD'S BEST SUGAR COOKIES
### Makes 2 to 3 dozen cookies

*My oldest daughter, Elizabeth, sometimes steps in to write "The Amish Cook" column for me if I am having a particularly busy week or I am sick. It seems readers enjoy hearing a younger voice from time to time. Elizabeth wrote a column for me in May 2008, and she included this recipe for sugar cookies in that column. It's an easy, soft cookie that also tastes great with Basic Frosting (see page 119) on top.*

1 cup powdered sugar

1 cup granulated sugar, plus more for pressing

1 cup (2 sticks) butter, softened

1 cup vegetable oil

2 teaspoons vanilla extract

2 large eggs

5 cups all-purpose flour

1 teaspoon salt

1 teaspoon baking soda

1 teaspoon cream of tartar

Basic Frosting (optional; see page 119)

Preheat the oven to 350°F.

In a large bowl, cream together the sugars, butter, oil, and vanilla until light and fluffy. Beat in the eggs. Sift the dry ingredients together in a bowl. Add to the creamed mixture and mix well.

Form the dough into balls on ungreased baking sheets and press flat to about a ½-inch thickness with a glass dipped in granulated sugar. Bake until the edges are golden, about 20 minutes. Frost the tops of the cookies after they cool if you like. Cool the cookies on a wire rack or a plate and then put into sealed containers. These cookies will stay fresh for up to 5 days.

## CHOCOLATE MARSHMALLOW COOKIES
### Makes 4½ dozen cookies

*This is a very soft cookie with an interesting mix of textures. They are great for an after-school snack!*

4 cups all-purpose flour

1 teaspoon baking soda

1 teaspoon salt

⅔ cup unsweetened cocoa powder

1 cup shortening, softened

2 cups granulated sugar

2 large eggs

2 teaspoons vanilla extract

1 cup thick sour milk

36 large marshmallows, cut in half

FROSTING:

6 tablespoons butter or margarine, melted

¼ cup unsweetened cocoa powder

1 teaspoon vanilla extract

3½ cups powdered sugar

5 to 6 tablespoons milk

Preheat the oven to 350°F. Lightly grease baking sheets and set aside.

In a medium bowl, stir together the flour, baking soda, salt, and cocoa powder. In another bowl, beat together the shortening, sugar, eggs, and vanilla until fluffy. Add the flour mixture to the shortening mixture alternately with the sour milk, mixing well after each addition.

Drop the batter by the teaspoonful onto the prepared baking sheets. Bake for 8 minutes. Top each cookie with a marshmallow half, and return to the oven for another 2 minutes to soften. Remove from the oven and cool the cookies on a wire rack or a plate and then put into sealed containers. These cookies will stay fresh for 2 days.

**To make the frosting:** In a medium bowl, combine all the ingredients and beat together until smooth. Once the cookies are cooled, spread the frosting over the tops, covering the marshmallows.

---

## OATMEAL COOKIES
### Makes 3 dozen cookies

*This is a very good oatmeal cookie. This recipe makes a softer cookie than the Overnight Oatmeal Cookies (see page 93). They are easy to mix and bake, and they are very easy for young bakers starting out to make. These cookies don't last very long in our household. These are good served right out of the oven. My children eat them with milk.*

1 cup margarine, softened

2 cups packed brown sugar

2 large eggs

2 teaspoons vanilla extract

2½ cups all-purpose flour

1 teaspoon salt

1½ teaspoons baking soda

3 cups quick-cooking rolled oats

2 cups granulated sugar

In a large bowl, cream together the margarine and brown sugar. Mix well, and then add the eggs and vanilla. Stir until the eggs are thoroughly blended in. Add the flour, salt, and baking soda. Stir until well blended. Add the oats and continue to vigorously stir until the oats are evenly blended. Chill the dough uncovered for several hours or overnight.

When ready to bake, preheat the oven to 350°F. Roll the dough into small balls about the size of a walnut. Pour the sugar into a shallow bowl and roll each ball through it, so that it's coated completely with sugar. Place on ungreased baking sheets and bake until edges and the tops of the cookie are golden brown, 18 to 20 minutes. The cookies will flatten while baking.

Cool the cookies on a wire rack or a plate and then put into sealed containers. These cookies will stay fresh for up to 7 days.

---

## SNICKERDOODLES

### Makes 3 dozen cookies

*Snickerdoodles have been around for as long as I can remember. They are just a plain cookie rolled in cinnamon and sugar just before baking. As a child, that name would always make me think of Snickers candy bars.*

1 cup shortening, softened

1½ cups plus 2 tablespoons sugar

2 large eggs

2¾ cups all-purpose flour

1 tablespoon cream of tartar

1 tablespoon salt

1 teaspoon baking soda

2 tablespoons ground cinnamon

Preheat the oven to 350°F.

Mix together the shortening, 1½ cups of the sugar, and the eggs. Stir in the flour, cream of tartar, salt, and baking soda. Chill the dough for at least 2 hours.

In a small bowl, combine the cinnamon and the remaining 2 tablespoons of sugar. Roll the dough into 1½-inch balls and roll into the cinnamon and sugar mixture. Place 2 inches apart on ungreased baking sheets and bake until the edges are golden brown, about 10 minutes. The cookies will spread out and flatten while they are baking. Cool the cookies on a wire rack or a plate and then put into sealed containers. These cookies will stay fresh for up to 5 days.

## $250 COOKIES

### Makes 10 dozen cookies

*This recipe uses a lot of oatmeal and nuts, which is why I think it is called "$250 Cookies." In some churches, this recipe is also known as a "bushel of cookies." These cookies, like the Church Cookies (see page 99), are passed around in church halfway through the services for the children to have a snack. Usually there are four or five different kinds of cookies to choose from after church. Oatmeal, chocolate chip, sugar, and molasses cookies are among the most popular. But there is usually a cookie like this among the mix.*

1 pound butter

2 cups granulated sugar

2 cups packed brown sugar

4 large eggs

2 teaspoons vanilla extract

4 cups all-purpose flour

5 cups quick-cooking rolled oats

1 teaspoon salt

1 teaspoon baking soda

1 teaspoon baking powder

1 (12-ounce) package semisweet chocolate chips

3 cups chopped nuts of your choice

1 (8-ounce) milk chocolate bar, grated

Preheat the oven to 375°F.

In a large bowl, cream together the butter and sugars. Stir in the eggs and vanilla. Mix in the flour, oatmeal, salt, baking soda, and baking powder until the oats are evenly mixed. Add the chocolate chips, nuts, and grated chocolate bar and mix to combine. Roll the dough into balls and place 2 inches apart on ungreased baking sheets. Bake until the edges of the cookies are golden, 8 to 10 minutes.

Cool the cookies on a wire rack or a plate and then put into sealed containers. These cookies will stay fresh for up to 7 days.

## WHOOPIE PIE HISTORY

Whoopie pies are another dessert closely identified with the Amish. The actual origins, however, are in dispute. Some food historians claim the cookie concoction is a Pennsylvania Dutch or Amish creation. Some old-timers in Maine believe the whoopie pie's roots are in New England. Either way, the Amish have embraced it as their own. The whoopie pie can be found in Amish-owned bakeries across the Midwest. Amish bakers have experimented with making the cookies in a variety of flavors, including pumpkin, peanut butter, chocolate, and spice. The cookie's name also has its share of stories, and one of the most popularly told among the Amish is that children would shout "Whoopie!" if they found one of these in their lunch pails.

## OATMEAL WHOOPIE PIE COOKIES

### Makes 24 whoopie pies

*It would be a real treat when we came home from school to discover Mom had made whoopie pies. Most people prepare these and then wrap them individually in plastic. This keeps them fresher and makes them easier to hand out to family and friends as treats.*

COOKIES:

¾ cup (1½ sticks) butter, softened

2 cups packed brown sugar

2 large eggs

½ teaspoon salt

2 cups all-purpose flour

1 teaspoon baking powder

1 teaspoon ground cinnamon

2 cups quick-cooking rolled oats

2 teaspoons baking soda

3 tablespoons boiling water

FILLING:

1 large egg white

1 tablespoon vanilla extract

2 tablespoons milk

2 cups powdered sugar

¼ cup shortening, softened

Preheat the oven to 425°F. Lightly grease a baking sheet and set aside.

**To make the cookies:** Cream the butter, sugar, and eggs in a large bowl. In a separate bowl, sift together the salt, flour, and baking powder. Add to the creamed mixture. Add the cinnamon and oats. Mix well. In a small dish, add the baking soda to the boiling water, and then stir the mixture into the rest of the batter. Mix well. Drop by the tablespoon onto the baking sheets about 2 inches apart and bake until the cookies are firm and just starting to turn golden around the edges, 10 to 15 minutes. Cool the cookies on a wire rack or a plate.

**To make the filling:** Combine the egg white, vanilla, milk, and 1 cup of the powdered sugar. Cream well. Add the remaining 1 cup of sugar and the shortening and beat until smooth. Spread 1 tablespoon of filling (more if desired) on one cookie, and then top with a second cookie.

Wrap each whoopie pie cookie in plastic wrap and then put into sealed containers. These cookies will stay fresh for up to 5 days.

## APPLE COOKIES

**Makes 4 dozen cookies**

*While I was growing up we had three apple trees in our front yard. My dad would always keep the trees pruned. And instead of spraying the trees for bugs, he would make equal amounts of lime, wood ash, and Epsom salts. He would put this around the trunks of the trees, and this would keep the bugs off the apples in an organic way with no spray. We like to make cookies like this with organically grown apples.*

¾ cup shortening, softened

1½ cups packed brown sugar

3 large eggs

1 teaspoon vanilla extract

2⅔ cups all-purpose flour

½ teaspoon salt

¾ teaspoon baking powder

¾ teaspoon baking soda

¾ teaspoon ground cinnamon

1½ cups quick-cooking rolled oats

2 medium McIntosh apples, peeled
    and chopped

¾ cup raisins

⅔ cup walnuts

Preheat the oven to 350°F. Grease baking sheets and set aside.

In a large bowl, cream together the shortening and brown sugar. Then add the eggs and beat the mixture until it's fluffy. Sift together 2 cups of the flour, the salt, baking powder, baking soda, and cinnamon. Add the sifted ingredients and the oats to the creamed mixture. Blend well.

In a separate bowl, stir together the remaining ⅓ cup of flour, the apples, raisins, and walnuts. Fold this mixture in with the rest of the batter. Drop by the teaspoon 2 inches apart onto the prepared baking sheets. Bake until edges are golden, about 12 minutes.

Cool the cookies on a wire rack or a plate and then put into sealed containers. These cookies will stay fresh for up to 5 days.

## DOUBLE-TREAT COOKIES

### Makes 8 dozen cookies

*In some Amish communities these are known as "Triple-Treat Cookies" because bakers add butterscotch chips to them. The treats in this cookie are peanuts and chocolate chips, but you can add a "triple" to this recipe with another sweet tidbit of your choosing.*

2 cups all-purpose flour

2 teaspoons baking soda

¼ teaspoon salt

1 cup shortening, softened

1 cup granulated sugar, plus more for shaping

1 cup packed brown sugar

2 large eggs

1 teaspoon vanilla extract

1 cup creamy peanut butter

1 cup chopped salted peanuts

1 (6-ounce package) semisweet chocolate chips

Preheat the oven to 350°F.

In a medium bowl, sift together the flour, baking soda, and salt. In a large bowl, beat together the shortening, sugars, eggs, and vanilla until fluffy. Blend in the peanut butter, and then add the dry ingredients. Stir in the peanuts and chocolate chips. Shape into small balls (about 1⅓ inches in diameter) and place 3 inches apart on ungreased baking sheets. Flatten with a glass dipped in granulated sugar and bake until brown, about 8 minutes. Let the cookies cool on the baking sheet before transferring to a plate.

Cool the cookies on a wire rack or a plate and then put into sealed containers. These cookies will stay fresh for up to 5 days.

## MAPLE DROP COOKIES

### Makes about 5 dozen cookies

*Maple flavorings are available at most bulk-food stores. The Amish-run bulk-food stores carry many different kinds of extracts and flavors, from peppermint to root beer. This cookie has a great taste of maple from the liquid flavoring.*

3½ cups all-purpose flour

1 teaspoon baking soda

Pinch of salt

1 cup (2 sticks) butter, softened

2 cups packed brown sugar

3 large eggs

¼ teaspoon maple flavoring

¼ cup walnut pieces

Preheat the oven to 375°F.

In a large bowl, combine the flour, baking soda, and salt. In a separate medium bowl, cream together the butter and sugar. Add the eggs one at a time, mixing well after each addition. Add the maple flavoring and walnuts. Stir vigorously until the batter is smooth and well blended. Gradually add the dry ingredients until well blended. The batter will be somewhat crumbly. Form into balls approximately 1 inch in size. Place on ungreased baking sheets. Bake until the edges are golden brown, 12 to 14 minutes. Let rest on the baking sheet for 2 to 3 minutes before transferring to a cooling rack.

Cool the cookies on a wire rack or a plate and then put into sealed containers. These cookies will stay fresh for up to 5 days.

## PINEAPPLE COOKIES

### Makes 3 dozen cookies

*My children enjoy the taste of pineapple, either by itself or when it's baked into something like these cookies. Mom would always have some pineapple on hand. Pineapple was first used a lot in different salads, but Amish bakers have found use for the fruit in a lot of different dishes, including breads and cookies.*

1 cup packed brown sugar

1 cup granulated sugar

2 large eggs

1 cup crushed pineapple, drained

1 teaspoon salt

3 teaspoons baking soda

1 teaspoon baking powder

4 cups all-purpose flour

Preheat the oven to 350°F.

In a large bowl, combine all of the ingredients together until smooth. Drop by the tablespoon 2 inches apart onto ungreased baking sheets and bake until the edges are golden brown, 15 to 20 minutes.

Cool the cookies on a wire rack or a plate and then put into sealed containers. These cookies will stay fresh for up to 5 days.

## CRYBABY COOKIES

### Makes about 3 dozen cookies

*Joe and I both like to drink coffee on occasion, although we try not to drink too much of it. Sometimes you wonder what to do with leftover coffee. I never like to just throw anything away. If you have leftover coffee, then this is a good recipe to use it up. These cookies have a good coffee flavor, but I'm not sure why they are called "crybabies."*

¾ cup shortening, softened

1 cup sugar

2 large eggs, beaten

1 cup molasses

4 cups all-purpose flour

¾ cup strong cold coffee

1 teaspoon salt

1 teaspoon baking soda

2 teaspoons ground cinnamon

2 teaspoons ground ginger

½ teaspoon ground cloves

Preheat the oven to 350°F. Grease baking sheets.

In a large bowl, mix all of the ingredients together until the dough forms a very thick batter. (This does not lend itself well to an electric mixer because it so thick.) Stir this vigorously with a wooden spoon. Use the spoon to mash the mixture against the side of the bowl if there are any bits of shortening not dissolved into the batter. Then resume stirring until all is mixed evenly. Drop by the teaspoon 2 inches apart onto the baking sheets. Bake until the edges are firm and slightly darker than the rest of the cookie, 10 to 15 minutes.

Cool the cookies on a wire rack or a plate and then put into sealed containers. These cookies will stay fresh for up to 3 days.

## CHILDREN'S BAKING
### Benjamin, 9

*I don't bake anything, but I always gather the eggs from the henhouse, so there are always eggs in the house for baking. My brother Joseph and I feed and water the chickens. We pick up all the eggs and take them to the house. When we let our chickens out we have to find all their hiding places where they lay their eggs. Some of the chickens even roost and lay eggs in the horse mangers. My mom says it's almost like having an Easter egg hunt every day. I don't bake but I always like to eat whatever gets baked at our house! I like these monster cookies the best!*

## MONSTER COOKIES
### Makes 6 dozen cookies

*My children like these cookies because of the M&M's. If these are in the pan when cookies are passed around at church, the children will grab these first because they see the M&M's. Mom would make these sometimes, not too often, because it was difficult to keep the M&M's on hand.*

1 cup (2 sticks) butter, softened
1 cup granulated sugar
1 cup packed brown sugar
3 large eggs
½ teaspoon vanilla extract
½ teaspoon corn syrup
2 teaspoons baking soda
1½ cups creamy peanut butter
4½ cups quick-cooking rolled oats
2 cups chocolate chips
2 cups plain M&M's

Preheat the oven to 350°F.

In a large bowl, cream the butter and sugars. Add the eggs, one at a time and mixing between each addition, the vanilla, corn syrup, baking soda, and peanut butter. Mix well until smooth. Add the oats and mix well, scraping the sides of the bowl. Add the chocolate chips and mix until they are evenly distributed throughout the batter. Then add the M&M's and mix well.

Drop the batter by the tablespoon 2 inches apart onto ungreased baking sheets. Bake until the edges are golden brown, 10 to 12 minutes. Let cool on baking sheets for about 3 minutes before transferring to cooling racks.

Cool the cookies on a wire rack or a plate and then put into sealed containers. These cookies will stay fresh for up to 5 days.

CAKES

# Chapter Four

*"In the winter, when it's cold outside, a homemade cake will last ten days.
In the summer, it might mold after a week. In families like ours, though,
there usually isn't any cake left over after that long anyway."*

— ELIZABETH COBLENTZ, 2001

Cakes are an important aspect of Amish culinary emotional expression. As noted earlier, emotional display is not a quality ingrained in Amish culture. Quite the opposite is true. Generations of Amish and Mennonites have been raised to embrace stoicism and strength as sought-after virtues. The Amish, as a culture, generally shy away from unnecessary frivolity. But food is expression among the Amish, and a cake is a canvas. Birthdays are commemorated with a bright, cheery sheet cake. For children, brightly colored candies—gumdrops or jelly beans—add extra emotion to the cake. For adults, candles caked in icing provide a flickering flame of celebration for another year passed.

Daughters who will one day become mothers learn the basics of baking under the watchful eyes of their mothers, a scene repeated for generations. Cakes are easy "mix and stir" stepping stones to bigger and better baking for aspiring young Amish homemakers. Many mothers start teaching their daughters the first bits of baking by simply having them grab a wooden spoon to mix up batter.

Amish-owned bakery cakes are filled with pound cakes, fruitcakes, marble cakes, and coffeecakes. There are funnel cakes and friendship cakes and funeral cakes. Virtually every occasion in Amish life, from birth to death, is observed within the frosting-filled confines of a cake.

One's harvest is also expressed easily in a cake. A bountiful season of carrots will show itself in cakes. Excess blueberries, beets, apples, rhubarb, strawberries, pears, and plums are just a few of the garden goodies that often find their way into a cake.

## LOVINA'S CAKES

There are so many ways cakes can be used for celebrations. When Joe and I were married, we had a nice four-layered wedding cake and two heart-shaped side cakes. Side cakes are decorative cakes that sit on the table next to the main wedding cake.

Cakes are always present at birthday celebrations, too. We always make sure the children have a cake with candles to blow out on their birthday. I used to be able to buy a 24-count box of candles and they would last for all the children. Now with everyone getting older, it takes more candles every year. To have enough candles for all the children's cakes now, I need 75 for a year. If you add Joe and me to that, then we need almost 150!

I have reused the candles if they haven't been burned down too much. The children don't seem to notice or care. They are too excited about blowing out the candles.

Another occasion when cakes are baked is when the children can take them to school to treat their classmates on their birthday, although most times I will make cupcakes instead, which are easier to pass out and the children don't need plates or forks.

There are some things that can be done to make sure your cakes come out okay and to make it less messy. For instance, a good way of avoiding getting your hands greasy when greasing your cake pan is to put your hand in a plastic sandwich bag and grease with that. Or just take a folded paper towel or napkin to spread the grease, which is how I do it most of the time. If you want to do more cupcakes than you have muffin pans for, try using canning jar rings to hold the papers in place on a baking sheet. Also, if a cake cracks on top it is usually because your oven is too hot or because the cake has too much flour added. A fallen cake can often be from underbaking or a too-low oven temperature. Dry, crumbly cakes often come from overbaking, overbeating, or too much flour. The most important ingredient to add to a cake is "fun"—they are made for enjoyment and celebration!

**BAKING TIP:**
Eggs will beat up fluffier if they are allowed to come to room temperature before beating.

## BASIC FROSTING
**Makes 2 cups**

*I use this recipe for anything that needs frosting: cakes, cinnamon rolls, Long John rolls, and even cookies. If you want a really white frosting, use shortening instead of butter. And if you want a certain color icing, just add a few drops of whatever food coloring you want.*

⅓ cup butter, softened
1 teaspoon vanilla extract
4 cups powdered sugar
½ cup milk

In a medium bowl, cream the butter with the vanilla and 1 cup of the powdered sugar. Gradually add the milk and the remaining powdered sugar and stir until smooth.

## RHUBARB CAKE
### Serves 8 to 12

*We love using fresh rhubarb in this cake recipe when the first tart stalks are ready in the spring. But this same recipe can be made using apples, strawberries, or whatever fruit is in season. This cake is also very good when served with an icing drizzled over it or topped with whipped cream.*

1¼ cups packed brown sugar

½ cup shortening, softened

1 large egg

2 cups all-purpose flour

½ teaspoon baking soda

½ teaspoon salt

1 cup buttermilk

1½ cups chopped fresh rhubarb

Whipped cream for serving (optional)

Preheat the oven to 350°F. Grease a 9 by 13-inch pan and set aside.

In a large bowl, combine the brown sugar, shortening, and egg. Beat until light and fluffy. In a separate bowl, blend the flour, baking soda, and salt. Add to the shortening mixture alternately with the buttermilk. Fold in the rhubarb. Spoon into the prepared pan and bake until a toothpick inserted into the middle comes out clean, about 35 minutes. Let the cake cool completely and store in a sealed container or cake safe. Top with whipped cream if desired. This cake will stay fresh for 3 to 4 days.

## RHUBARB SHORTCAKE

**Serves 6 to 8**

*When I was growing up, we would have rhubarb shortcake a lot of times right out of the oven for supper in the evenings. We would sprinkle sugar and cold milk on top. We never had it for breakfast unless it was left over. My dad wouldn't put milk on it; he would just eat it warm. I have fixed rhubarb shortcake for my children many times, and some like it more than others. If we have ice cream in the freezer, they would prefer that ice cream be served with it. We never had that choice growing up. They don't act like they care for the milk on the rhubarb like I did when I was younger. The children do really like rhubarb juice and jam.*

4 cups all-purpose flour

1 teaspoon baking soda

2 teaspoons baking powder

Pinch of salt

3 cups sour milk

2 cups chopped rhubarb

1 cup sugar

Preheat the oven to 350°F.

In a large bowl, combine the flour, baking soda, baking powder, and salt. Then gradually add the sour milk until a really soft dough forms. Spread a layer of this dough in a 9 by 13-inch cake pan, and then add a thick layer of rhubarb. Put the sugar on the rhubarb. Put rest of the dough on top and bake until the rhubarb is tender, about 45 minutes.

## APPLESAUCE CAKE
### Serves 8 to 12

*We had a Yellow Transparent tree in our front yard when I was growing up. We also had a McIntosh and a Jonathan tree. The Jonathan is a good eating apple, while the McIntosh is good for cooking and baking. But with the yellow apples, Mom always used to make applesauce. I would always get my apples for applesauce off my mom and dad's tree if I needed more. My children like applesauce with cake or cookies, so this recipe is a big hit in our house.*

1 cup sugar

1 cup salad dressing (Miracle Whip)

½ cup milk

2 cups unsweetened applesauce

1 teaspoon vanilla extract

3 cups all-purpose flour

2 teaspoons baking soda

2 teaspoons ground cinnamon

½ teaspoon ground nutmeg

½ teaspoon ground allspice

½ teaspoon salt

Preheat the oven to 350°F. Grease and flour a 9 by 13-inch pan and set aside.

In a large bowl, cream together the sugar, salad dressing, and milk. Beat in the applesauce and vanilla. In a separate bowl, combine the flour, baking soda, cinnamon, nutmeg, allspice, and salt. Add the dry ingredients, a little at a time, to the wet mixture. The batter will be thick and slightly lumpy. Pour into the prepared pan and bake until a toothpick inserted in the center comes out clean, 35 to 40 minutes.

Let the cake cool completely and store in a sealed container or cake safe. This cake will stay fresh for 3 days.

## PEANUT BUTTER CAKE

**Serves 8 to 12**

*Everyone in my family likes peanut butter: Peanut butter spread, peanut butter cookies, and so on. My children will eat just plain peanut butter on bread, or on celery sticks.*

CAKE:

¼ cup margarine, softened

¾ cup creamy peanut butter

1½ cup packed brown sugar

2 large eggs

½ cup warm water

1 cup buttermilk

2 cups all-purpose flour

1 teaspoon salt

1 teaspoon baking soda

PEANUT BUTTER FROSTING:

1 cup semisweet chocolate chips, melted

2 tablespoons margarine, softened

5 tablespoons creamy peanut butter

2 cups powdered sugar

½ teaspoon vanilla extract

3 to 4 tablespoons milk

Preheat the oven to 350°F. Grease and flour a 9 by 13-inch pan and set aside.

**To make the cake:** In a large bowl, blend the margarine, peanut butter, and brown sugar until thick and creamy in consistency. Add the eggs, water, buttermilk, flour, salt, and baking soda. Mix until creamy and thoroughly blended. Spoon into the prepared pan and bake until a toothpick comes out clean, 25 to 30 minutes.

Let the cake cool completely and store in a sealed container or cake safe. This cake will stay fresh for 3 to 4 days.

**To make the frosting:** Blend together all the frosting ingredients until thick and creamy in a medium bowl. Spread on the cooled cake.

## CHOCOLATE CHIP CAKE
**Serves 10**

*This is a moist, classic chocolate cake that can be used to celebrate birthdays or a child's accomplishments at school. Be sure to spread the chocolate chips evenly over the top of the batter.*

1¾ cups flour

1 teaspoon baking soda

1 teaspoon salt

2 tablespoons unsweetened cocoa powder

1 cup shortening

1 cup sugar

2 large eggs, beaten

1 teaspoon vanilla extract

1 cup boiling water

6 ounces chocolate chips

Preheat the oven to 350°F. Lightly grease a 9 by 13-inch pan and set aside.

In a large bowl, sift together the flour, baking soda, salt, and cocoa. Set aside. In a separate large bowl, cream together the shortening and sugar. Add the eggs and vanilla to the shortening mixture. Beat thoroughly. Add the boiling water and the flour mixture alternately to the shortening mixture, mixing batter until smooth after each addition. The mixture will be smooth and creamy.

Spoon and spread into the prepared pan. Sprinkle the batter evenly with the chocolate chips. Bake until the cake is firm, about 45 minutes.

Let the cake cool completely and store in a sealed container or cake safe. This cake will stay fresh for 3 to 4 days.

## PLUM CAKE
**Serves 8 to 12**

*Mom would often order a bushel of plums. A truck would come to an Amish farm nearby and he would deliver peaches, apples, plums, or any fruit you wanted. Mom would order a bushel and can them. We'd open a can of plums just like we would a can of peaches or cherries, and that would be another fruit for us to experience. We would eat them with cake or cookies and mix the fruits all together. With peaches the pits were out already, but with the plums they were not, so we had to be careful when we ate them.*

CAKE:
1 cup vegetable oil
1½ cups sugar
3 large eggs
2 cups all-purpose flour
1 teaspoon baking powder
1 teaspoon baking soda

½ teaspoon salt
1 teaspoon ground cinnamon
½ teaspoon ground nutmeg
½ teaspoon ground allspice
1 cup thick sour milk or buttermilk
1 cup cooked, chopped plums, drained
¾ cup chopped walnuts

GLAZE:
½ cup sugar
¼ cup thick sour milk or buttermilk
1 tablespoon light corn syrup
2 tablespoons butter
¼ teaspoon baking soda
½ teaspoon vanilla extract

Preheat the oven to 350°F. Grease and flour a 9 by 13-inch pan and set aside.

**To make the cake:** In a large bowl, combine the vegetable oil, sugar, eggs, flour, baking powder, and baking soda until the mixture is smooth and creamy. Then stir in the salt, cinnamon, nutmeg, allspice, sour milk, plums, and walnuts. Stir until the fruits and nuts are evenly distributed throughout the batter. Pour into the prepared pan and bake until a toothpick inserted in the center comes out clean, 35 to 40 minutes.

Let the cake cool completely and store in a sealed container or cake safe. This cake will stay fresh for 3 to 4 days.

**To make the glaze:** Combine the sugar, sour milk, corn syrup, butter, baking soda, and vanilla in a small saucepan and cook over medium heat, stirring constantly until the mixture boils. Turn the heat to low and boil for 5 minutes, stirring occasionally. Remove from the heat. Cool the cake for 5 minutes, and then make deep holes in it with a fork so that the glaze will soak into the cake. Pour the glaze over the hot cake.

## "FROM-SCRATCH CAKES"

Amish bulk-food stores are full of bagged cake mixes to make your own cakes. And of course the supermarkets have plenty of boxed cake mixes. But I like making my own from scratch. Here are some easy mixes that you can use for all your cakes.

## BASIC CAKE MIX
### Serves 15

*This is an easy mix for a basic cake. I remember one spring, I bought a horseshoe-shaped cake pan at a garage sale. The children were eager to see how a cake shaped like a horseshoe would look, so my daughter Elizabeth made one, frosted it, and lined the edges with chocolate chips. Needless to say, the children were all excited to see it and eat it. All we had the following summer were horseshoe-shaped cakes, often made with this mix.*

9½ cups all-purpose flour

6 cups sugar

¼ cup baking powder

1 tablespoon salt

2½ cups shortening, softened

In a large bowl, sift together the flour, sugar, baking powder, and salt and add the softened shortening. Cut in until the mixture resembles very fine crumbs. Divide the mix into 4 equal portions of 4½ cups each. Place in airtight containers and store in a cool, dry place for up to 2 months. Or place in freezer containers and freeze for up to 6 months.

**To use:** Allow the mix to come to room temperature.

## YELLOW CAKE FROM MIX

**4 ½ cups Basic Cake Mix (page 127)**
**1 cup milk**
**1 teaspoon vanilla extract**
**2 large eggs**

Preheat the oven to 350°F. Grease and flour a 9 by 13-inch pan and set aside.

In a bowl, combine all the ingredients. Beat until moistened, 1 to 2 minutes. Pour into the prepared pan and bake until a toothpick inserted in the center comes out clean, about 25 minutes.

*White cake from mix:* Prepare the batter as for the yellow cake, but use 3 egg whites instead of 2 whole eggs.

*Chocolate cake from mix:* Follow the ingredients as for the yellow cake, but add ¼ cup unsweetened cocoa powder.

*Spice cake from mix:* Follow the recipe as for a yellow cake, except add 1 teaspoon ground cinnamon, ¼ teaspoon ground allspice, and ¼ teaspoon ground cloves.

## LAZY WOMAN'S CAKE

### Serves 6 to 8

*This also makes good cupcakes. The cake has a funny name, but if you have a houseful of children like I do, sometimes a lazy cake is just the answer when dessert is needed in a pinch!*

2 cups sugar

3 cups all-purpose flour

1 teaspoon salt

5 tablespoons unsweetened cocoa powder

2 heaping teaspoons baking soda

1 cup vegetable oil

1 tablespoon vanilla extract

2 tablespoons vinegar

2 cups cold water

Preheat the oven to 350°F.

In a large bowl, combine all the ingredients. Mix until the batter is creamy and smooth. Pour into an ungreased 9 by 13-inch pan and bake until a toothpick inserted in the center comes out clean, about 30 minutes.

Let the cake cool completely and store in a sealed container or cake safe. This cake will stay fresh for 3 to 4 days.

## EGGLESS CAKE
### Serves 6 to 8

*Often eggs are needed when baking a cake, especially if you want it to be nice and moist. This is another cake (besides the Lazy Woman's Cake, page 129) that doesn't require eggs but still makes a nice, moist chocolate cake.*

2 cups granulated sugar

½ cup vegetable oil

1 cup buttermilk

1 teaspoon vanilla extract

Dash of salt

3 tablespoons unsweetened cocoa powder

2¾ cups all-purpose flour

1 cup water

2 teaspoons baking soda

CARAMEL ICING:

4 tablespoons (½ stick) butter

½ cup packed brown sugar

2 tablespoons milk

1¾ cups powdered sugar

Preheat the oven to 350°F. Grease and flour a 9 by 13-inch pan and set aside.

In a large bowl, mix the sugar, oil, buttermilk, vanilla, salt, cocoa, and flour until evenly mixed. In a small saucepan, heat the water to boiling. Remove from the heat and add the baking soda. Pour the mixture into the batter and mix until smooth. Pour into the prepared pan and bake until a toothpick inserted in the center comes out clean, about 35 minutes.

**To make the icing:** Stir together the butter and brown sugar in a small saucepan, and bring to a boil over low heat. Remove from the heat and add the milk and powdered sugar. Stir until smooth and spread onto the cake.

Let the cake cool completely and store in a sealed container or cake safe. This cake will stay fresh for 3 to 4 days.

## AMISH CULTURAL INSIGHT: WHAT IS A FROLIC?

Among the Amish, a frolic is when a lot of people gather to help you for the day. A barn-raising is considered a "frolic," but so is putting up a fence, a shed, or framing for your house. If you need help for the day, you tell everyone that you are going to have a frolic and most that can will come and help. When we built our new house, we had a frolic to do the framing. One Saturday the church men all came to help frame the walls. In return for their help, we fed them a meal and Joe later returned the help.

Since we have lived in Michigan, Joe has probably been invited to ten or twelve frolics. They announce it in front of the church, and if somebody wants to have a really big one he'll announce it in front of all the area churches. There are also frolics for the women, which will be days of sewing, cleaning, or baking.

When we had our frolic we had one of the men serve as the "crew leader" for the day. Since Joe was going to be busy getting supplies and watching the progress of the work, the crew leader was the one who had the stress of keeping all the men busy. That can be a full-time job. The crew leader put in a long day, but it was all free labor. Our church always seems to come together to pitch in when someone really needs help.

The type of meal served at a frolic really depends on how many people show up. For our frolic, we had barbecued chicken and mashed potatoes and gravy, just a regular big meal. Some of the women sent along desserts with their husbands. At some places wives will also go along to help. When the Jacobs had a barn frolic, 30 or 40 men showed up, so some of the women went along to help with the cooking. Cakes, cookies, and pies are among the baked goods brought to a frolic.

I remember going to a barn-raising frolic as a girl. I think they were building a new barn; I don't think it had burned down. There were so many men there and a lot of women. The men were all over the barn roof. They were just started with the frame when we got there that morning, and they were finishing the roof in the evening. Buckets, towels, and washbasins for the men to get cleaned up were there, and the meal was outside. The men just kind of sat out in the yard and ate. For us children, it was fun just to sit and watch. There were a lot of dishes to wash when it was over, though!

## PEACH UPSIDE-DOWN CAKE

**Serves 6 to 8**

*My children eat and enjoy home-canned peaches. While we don't have a peach tree in our yard, we do make sure we get plenty of peaches each year when they are in season. A lady in church will usually have a truck unload them at her place, and everyone has to go pick up their bushels of peaches from there. I ordered several bushels one year. I like to order at least one bushel every year, but if prices aren't too bad I order more. In addition to the home-canned peaches, the children like to also just eat them fresh. Peaches can also be enjoyed in jams and baked goods like this upside-down cake. Most around here would use homegrown, home-canned peaches. But you can use store-bought for this recipe.*

| | |
|---|---|
| 1 quart canned sliced peaches | 2 large eggs |
| 6 tablespoons margarine or butter | 2 teaspoons vanilla extract |
| 1 cup packed brown sugar | 2½ teaspoons baking powder |
| ⅔ cup vegetable shortening | 1 teaspoon salt |
| 1 cup granulated sugar | 2 cups all-purpose flour |

Preheat the oven to 350°F. Grease a 9 by 13-inch cake pan and set aside.

Drain the peaches and reserve the syrup. Melt the butter in a large skillet. Add the brown sugar, 2 tablespoons of the peach syrup, and the drained peaches to the skillet. Let simmer over low heat. Add enough water to the remaining peach syrup to make 1 cup, and set aside.

In a large bowl, cream together the shortening and granulated sugar until light and crumbly. Add the eggs and vanilla. Beat until fluffy. In a separate medium bowl, sift together the baking powder, salt, and flour. Add the dry mixture and the 1 cup of syrup alternately to the creamed mixture, stirring after each addition until smooth. The batter will be thick, a bit heavier than a cake batter.

Remove the skillet from the heat and, using a slotted spoon, remove the peaches from the skillet and spread the fruit in the bottom of the prepared cake pan.

Spread the batter evenly over the peaches and bake until the top is brown and a toothpick inserted in the center comes out clean, 35 to 40 minutes.

Let the cake cool completely and store in a sealed container or cake safe. This cake will stay fresh for 3 to 4 days.

## OLD-FASHIONED BLUEBERRY CAKE
### Serves 6 to 8

*We have several blueberry "U-pick" patches around. My sister, Emma, and Jacob and their children usually go every year and give me some fresh blueberries. You can freeze blueberries well as long as you don't wash them before freezing. They shouldn't have any water on them when going into the freezer.*

1 pint blueberries (2 cups fresh or frozen)

1 cup plus 2 tablespoons sugar

1½ cups plus 1 tablespoon all-purpose flour

Grated lemon zest from 2 lemons

9 tablespoons butter, softened

¾ teaspoon baking powder

¾ teaspoon baking soda

¼ teaspoon ground cinnamon

Dash of salt

2 large eggs, at room temperature

½ teaspoon vanilla extract

⅔ cup sour cream

Pinch of ground nutmeg

Preheat the oven to 350°F. Grease a 2-quart ovenproof casserole dish or a 9-inch square pan.

In a large bowl, combine the blueberries with ½ cup of the sugar, 1 tablespoon of the flour, and 2 teaspoons of the lemon zest and place in the prepared casserole dish. Cut in 2 tablespoons of the butter and toss. Bake for 10 minutes. Stir gently after removing from the oven.

While the berries are baking, sift together the remaining 1½ cups of flour, the baking powder, baking soda, cinnamon, salt, and 1 tablespoon of the lemon zest. Set aside.

In a separate bowl, cream 6 tablespoons of the butter with ½ cup of the sugar. Add the eggs one at a time and beat until well blended. Blend in 1 teaspoon of the lemon zest and the vanilla. Add the flour mixture and the sour cream alternately to the egg mixture, starting with the flour and ending with the sour cream and combining after each addition.

Drop the batter by spoonfuls over the baked berries, spreading evenly. Combine the remaining 2 tablespoons sugar, the nutmeg, ¼ teaspoon lemon zest, and the remaining 1 tablespoon butter. Crumble over the top of the batter. Bake until a toothpick inserted in the center of the cake comes out clean, about 35 minutes.

Let the cake cool completely and store in a sealed container or cake safe. This cake will stay fresh for 3 to 4 days.

## HOT MILK SPONGE CAKE

### Serves 6 to 8

*This is an old recipe that is simple and easy to make. It has a good, sweet taste that goes over well in this household!*

2 cups cake flour

2 teaspoons baking powder

½ teaspoon salt

4 large eggs

2 teaspoons vanilla extract

2 cups sugar

1 cup milk

1 tablespoon butter

Preheat the oven to 350°F. Grease a 9 by 13-inch pan, flour only the bottom, and set aside.

In a large bowl, sift together the flour, baking powder, and salt. In another large bowl, beat the eggs and vanilla together. Then gradually add the sugar and continue beating until the mixture becomes light and lemon-colored. Blend the dry ingredients into the creamed mixture. Bring the milk and butter to the boiling point. Then quickly stir into the batter and blend well. Pour quickly into the prepared baking pan. Bake until the cake is set, 35 to 40 minutes.

Let the cake cool completely and store in a sealed container or cake safe. This cake will stay fresh for 3 to 4 days.

## SOUR CREAM SPICE CAKE
### Serves 6 to 8

*Mom didn't ever buy sour cream. We had a plentiful supply of sour milk and buttermilk, which could be used in recipes like these. Her homemade sour cream also tasted so good and added a lot of flavor to a cake like this. Since most people wouldn't make their own, you can use store-bought for this cake and it'll still taste nice and moist.*

½ cup shortening, softened

2 cups packed brown sugar

1 cup sour cream

1¾ cups all-purpose flour

3 large eggs, separated

1 tablespoon baking soda

1 tablespoon cloves, crushed

1 teaspoon ground allspice

½ teaspoon salt

1 teaspoon vanilla extract

Preheat the oven to 350°F. Lightly grease and set aside a 5 by 9-inch loaf pan.

In a large bowl, cream together the shortening and sugar. Add the sour cream and mix well. Then add the flour, egg yolks, baking soda, cloves, allspice, and salt. Stir in the vanilla. Beat the egg whites until stiff and then fold them into the mixture. Bake in the prepared pan until a toothpick inserted in the center comes out clean, about 30 minutes.

Let the cake cool completely and store in a sealed container or cake safe. This cake will stay fresh for 3 to 4 days.

## MARBLE CAKE
### Serves 6 to 8

*Cakes are needed for so many different occasions around here that sometimes it is nice to bring something to a gathering that is a little different. This is a good, moist cake and a nice change from a plain chocolate cake. More chocolate added, though, makes it more "marbled/gooey" and can be done if that is your preference. If you like, sprinkle powdered sugar over the cake and serve warm, or let it cool and ice it with chocolate frosting.*

| | |
|---|---|
| 2½ cups all-purpose flour | 1 cup semisweet chocolate chips, melted |
| 1½ teaspoons baking powder | 2 tablespoons hot water |
| 1¾ teaspoons baking soda | ¾ cup shortening, softened |
| 1 teaspoon salt | 1 cup sour milk or buttermilk |
| 1⅔ cups plus 1 tablespoon sugar | 2 large eggs |

Preheat the oven to 350°F. Grease a 9 by 13-inch pan and set aside.

In a bowl, mix together the flour, baking powder, 1½ teaspoons of the baking soda, the salt, and 1⅔ cups of the sugar. Set aside. In another bowl, combine the melted chocolate, hot water, remaining ¼ teaspoon baking soda, and remaining 1 tablespoon sugar. Mix well and set aside.

In a large bowl, put the softened shortening. Add the flour mixture and sour milk into the shortening alternately, stirring after each addition. Add the eggs and mix well. The batter will be slightly thick.

Remove about one-quarter of the batter (1¼ cups), add to the chocolate mixture, and mix well. Alternately spoon the plain and chocolate batters into the prepared pan. Then, with a knife, cut through the batter in a wide zigzag course until the desired marbling is reached. Bake until a toothpick inserted an inch from the center comes out clean, 35 to 40 minutes. Cover with aluminum foil after 20 minutes of baking to prevent the top from overbrowning.

Let the cake cool completely and store in a sealed container or cake safe. This cake will stay fresh for 3 to 4 days.

## AMISH ANGEL FOOD CAKE

**Serves 12**

*Angel food cakes are a great light dessert during the hot summer months, which is when our family really enjoys them. Also, angel food cakes are often prepared for weddings around here and put on the guests' tables. Pie filling is often drizzled on the cake. You could also serve it with fruit and whipped cream, or drizzled with icing. I really like angel food cake, and I would go for that before other flavors of cake.*

1¼ cups cake flour

1¾ cups sugar

1½ cups egg whites (from 8 to 11 eggs, depending on size)

1½ teaspoons cream of tartar

1 teaspoon vanilla extract

¼ teaspoon salt

Preheat the oven to 375°F.

Mix together the flour and ¾ cup of the sugar. Divide into 4 equal parts and set aside.

In a large bowl, beat the egg whites, cream of tartar, vanilla, and salt until foamy. It would be best to use a rotary hand mixer (or an electric mixer, if accessible). Beat in the remaining 1 cup sugar, 2 tablespoons at a time. Stir vigorously for several minutes until the meringue holds stiff peaks that are glossy and moist. With a rubber spatula, gently fold each of the 4 portions of the flour mixture into the meringue, gently folding after each addition until the flour and sugar mixture disappears.

Scrape the batter into an ungreased 10-inch tube pan. Gently cut through the batter once with a spatula to remove air bubbles. Do not lift the spatula out of the batter while doing this. Bake until the cake springs back when lightly touched with a finger and a long wooden toothpick inserted halfway between the sides comes out clean, 35 to 40 minutes. Invert the pan over a cooling rack and let the cake cool before removing.

Let the cake cool completely and store in a sealed container or cake safe. This cake will stay fresh for 3 to 4 days.

## RED BEET CHOCOLATE SHEET CAKE
**Serves 8 to 12**

*I was reluctant to try this cake, as I had a hard time associating red beets with chocolate. I love pickled red beets, but other than that I am not too fond of red beets. But when I took my first bite of this cake I was amazed by the taste. It is a very moist cake and you cannot taste the red beets. Neither can you taste the chocolate chips that were added. My daughter Elizabeth doesn't care for red beets at all either, but she agreed that you couldn't taste the beets. She said this is probably the only way she could eat red beets. I gave my youngest children a piece, and they really went for it. This is not a cake you eat warm, so let it cool completely before serving.*

1¾ cups all-purpose flour

½ teaspoon salt

½ teaspoon baking soda

1½ cups granulated sugar

3 large eggs

1 cup vegetable oil

1½ cups cooked and pureed fresh beets

1 cup semisweet chocolate chips

1 teaspoon vanilla extract

Sifted powdered sugar for sprinkling

Preheat the oven to 350°F. Butter a 9 by 13-inch cake pan and set aside.

Mix together the flour, salt, and baking soda and set aside. Combine the sugar, eggs, and oil in a large bowl. Stir vigorously (those who use electric mixers can use one here on medium speed for 2 minutes). Beat in the beets, melted chocolate, and vanilla.

Gradually add the dry ingredients to the beet mixture, beating well after each addition. Pour into the prepared pan. Bake until a toothpick inserted into the center of the cake comes out clean, 40 to 45 minutes. Cool in the pan. Cover and let stand overnight to improve the flavor. Sprinkle with powdered sugar.

Let the cake cool completely and store in a sealed container or cake safe. This cake will stay fresh for 3 to 4 days.

## PINEAPPLE SHEET CAKE

**Serves 12**

*This is an easy, sweet cake that will appeal to pineapple lovers. Sometimes it is served with the other desserts after Sunday church services.*

CAKE:

1 (20-ounce) can crushed pineapple, drained

2 teaspoons baking soda

¼ cup water

1 teaspoon vanilla extract

2 large eggs, beaten

2 cups granulated sugar

2 cups all-purpose flour

FROSTING:

½ cup margarine, softened

1 (8-ounce) package cream cheese

1 teaspoon vanilla extract

2 cups powdered sugar

Preheat the oven to 350°F. Grease a 10 by 15-inch sheet cake pan and set aside.

**To make the cake:** In a large bowl, stir the pineapple, baking soda, water, and vanilla until the ingredients are well blended. Add the eggs and mix until blended. Slowly add the sugar and flour, scraping down the sides of the bowl when necessary to ensure the mixture is evenly blended. The batter will be a medium yellow color and slightly bubbly. Spoon the batter into the prepared pan. Bake until the cake pulls away from the edges of the pan and is golden brown, about 30 minutes. A knife inserted in the center will come out clean. Remove from the oven and let cool.

**To make the frosting:** Stir the softened margarine in a small bowl for about a minute until smooth, and then add the cream cheese. Blend together for several minutes, and then add the vanilla. After the vanilla is thoroughly mixed in, add the powdered sugar, ½ cup at a time, scraping down the sides of the bowl frequently and mixing until the frosting is smooth. Spread evenly over the warm cake.

Let the cake cool completely and store in a sealed container or cake safe. This cake will stay fresh for 3 to 4 days.

## MOLASSES CAKE

### Serves 12

*Molasses always reminds me of honey. I'm not sure if it is because they are both sticky to handle. If a recipe calls for molasses and I don't have any, I'll substitute honey, and vice-versa. This cake can be enjoyed with Basic Frosting (see page 119) or without.*

2 cups all-purpose flour

¾ cup molasses

¼ cup sugar

2 teaspoons baking soda

1 large egg

½ cup buttermilk or sour milk

½ cup hot water

Preheat the oven to 350°F. Lightly grease a 9 by 13-inch pan and set aside.

In a large bowl, combine all the ingredients. Mix thoroughly. Spoon into the prepared pan. Bake until the cake is firm and a toothpick inserted into the center comes out clean, about 40 minutes.

Let the cake cool completely and store in a sealed container or cake safe. This cake will stay fresh for 3 to 4 days.

## PEAR CAKE
### Serves 6 to 8

*At my parents' house there used to be a pear tree out by the garden. That is how I learned to like pears. If any of us children were hungry for an afternoon snack we'd just go out to the pear tree and grab one, take it to the water pump to wash it, and then just eat it. We had a little shed right next to the pear tree where we had our dolls and playhouse, so I have good memories of pears. I and most people I know would use home-canned pears for this recipe, but for those of you who don't have them, the recipe has been changed to use store-bought canned pears. This is delicious served with a scoop of vanilla ice cream.*

CAKE:

1½ cups vegetable oil

2 cups sugar

3 large eggs

3 cups all-purpose flour

1 teaspoon salt

1 teaspoon ground cinnamon

1 teaspoon baking soda

1 teaspoon vanilla extract

1 cup pecans, finely chopped

2 cups pears (15¼-ounce can in heavy syrup), chopped and drained (reserve syrup)

GLAZE:

1 tablespoon butter, softened

1½ cups powdered sugar

3 tablespoons syrup from the pears

Preheat the oven to 325°F. Grease a Bundt or tube pan.

**To make the cake:** In a large bowl, combine the oil, sugar, and eggs. Beat until creamy. In a medium bowl, sift together the flour, salt, cinnamon, and baking soda. Stir the dry ingredients into the creamed mixture until smooth. Add the vanilla. Fold in the pecans and pears. Pour the mixture into the prepared pan. Bake until a toothpick inserted into the center comes out clean, about 1 hour and 15 minutes.

**To make the glaze:** Blend the butter and sugar. Add the pear syrup and stir until well mixed and slightly runny. Drizzle over the cake.

Let the cake cool completely and store in a sealed container or cake safe. This cake will stay fresh for 3 to 4 days.

## PUMPKIN SHEET CAKE
Serves 12

*Pumpkin is something we grow in the garden some years. When Benjamin saved seeds from a pumpkin one year, he wrapped them in paper towels to dry out and then put them in one of my kitchen drawers. He would keep asking me, when is it time to plant the seeds in the garden? When garden planting season came around he didn't forget, and he was there with his seeds. We did get a few little pumpkins from the seeds, of which he was very proud. This is a good cake for enjoying the taste of pumpkin. Basic Frosting (see page 119) can be added if desired, or it is tasty plain. I would use a home-canned pumpkin for this, but store bought would work okay, too.*

2 cups sugar

4 large eggs

1 cup vegetable oil

2 cups all-purpose flour

1 cup nuts of your choice

2 cups pureed pumpkin

½ teaspoon salt

1 teaspoon baking soda

2 teaspoons baking powder

2 teaspoons ground cinnamon or pumpkin pie spice

Preheat the oven to 350°F.

In a large bowl, combine all the ingredients until the mixture is evenly and thoroughly combined. Spoon into a 10 by 15-inch pan. Bake until a toothpick inserted in the center comes out clean, about 30 minutes.

Let the cake cool completely and store in a sealed container or cake safe. This cake will stay fresh for 3 to 4 days.

## BLUEBERRY STREUSEL COFFEECAKE
**Serves 12**

*Nuts, especially pecans, would make a nice addition to the streusel. Our family enjoys a warm coffeecake on a cold winter's morning.*

**STREUSEL:**

½ cup graham cracker crumbs

2 tablespoons sugar

½ teaspoon ground cinnamon

4 tablespoons (½ stick) butter or
  margarine, softened

**COFFEECAKE:**

2 cups all-purpose flour

3 teaspoons baking powder

1 teaspoon salt

¼ cup sugar

4 tablespoons (½ stick) butter or margarine,
  softened

½ cup milk

1 large egg, beaten

1½ cups fresh blueberries (or thawed and
  drained frozen)

Preheat the oven to 400°F. Grease and flour a 9-inch round layer cake pan and set aside.

**To make the streusel:** In a medium bowl, mix the graham cracker crumbs, sugar, and cinnamon. Cut in the butter as for a pie dough until it is the texture of small peas. Set the streusel aside.

**To make the coffeecake:** In a large bowl, mix the flour, baking powder, salt, and sugar. Cut in the butter until the mixture is the consistency of coarse cornmeal. Make a well in the center and pour in the milk. Add the egg and stir quickly with a fork just until the dry ingredients are moistened. Spread the batter in the prepared pan. Arrange the berries over the batter, leaving a 1-inch margin around the edge of the pan. Sprinkle the streusel over the berries. Bake until the top is nicely browned, about 30 minutes.

Let the cake cool completely and store in a sealed container or cake safe. This cake will stay fresh for 3 to 4 days.

## HONEY NUT SWIRL COFFEECAKE

### Serves 6 to 8

*This recipe is perfect for people who love nuts. This coffeecake tastes kind of like a sweet roll with nuts. This recipe can be challenging and requires a bit of effort, but it is well worth the work.*

| | |
|---|---|
| 1 cup milk | **FILLING:** |
| ½ cup shortening | 2 large eggs |
| ½ cup sugar | ½ cup honey |
| 2 teaspoons salt | 4 tablespoons (½ stick) butter, melted |
| 2 packages active dry yeast | 3 cups chopped nuts of your choice |
| 1 cup warm water | 2 teaspoons ground cinnamon |
| 2 large eggs | 1 teaspoon vanilla extract |
| 6 cups all-purpose flour | |

In a small saucepan, scald the milk over low heat, about 3 minutes. Remove the milk from the heat. Add the shortening, sugar, and salt to the saucepan and stir. In a large bowl, dissolve the yeast in the warm water, about 5 minutes. Add the milk mixture, eggs, and 2 cups of the flour to the yeast. Beat until smooth. Gradually add the rest of the flour to make the dough soft. Turn out the dough onto a lightly floured cutting board. Let rise for 10 minutes, uncovered, on the cutting board. Place in a greased bowl. Cover and let rise in a warm place until double in size, about 2 hours.

Punch the dough down and let it rise again for about 1 hour.

**While the dough is rising, make the filling:** Mix the eggs, honey, butter, nuts, cinnamon, and vanilla until smooth and creamy. Divide the dough in half. Roll each half into 12 by 18-inch rectangles. Spread each half with the filling. Starting with the short side, roll up each sheet as for a jelly roll. Put the rolled-up dough lengthwise on a 10 by 15-inch jelly-roll pan. Let rise for 30 minutes.

While the dough is rising, preheat the oven to 350°F. Bake until the top turns golden brown, about 45 minutes. Let the cake cool completely and store in a sealed container or cake safe. This cake will stay fresh for 3 to 4 days.

## CHERRY COFFEECAKE
**Serves 6 to 8**

*I remember that Mother would always can quart after quart of cherries. She would order a big batch of cherries and make cherry pie filling and can the rest. When she would open a quart we would eat them just like we would canned peaches. But the cherries she would can wouldn't be pitted, so when we ate them we would have to make sure we didn't swallow the seeds.*

CAKE:
1 cup (2 sticks) butter or margarine, softened
1½ cups granulated sugar
4 large eggs, beaten
1 teaspoon vanilla extract

3 cups all-purpose flour
1½ teaspoons baking powder
½ teaspoon salt
21 ounces cherry pie filling

GLAZE:
3 tablespoons butter
2½ cups powdered sugar
1 teaspoon vanilla extract
6 tablespoons milk

Preheat the oven to 350°F.

**To make the cake:** In a medium bowl, cream the butter until smooth (about 1 minute). Gradually add the sugar and continue stirring until the mixture is a creamy, pale yellow. Add the beaten eggs into the sugar mixture in four additions, stirring vigorously for about 1 minute after each addition. Stir in the vanilla. In a separate medium bowl, sift the flour, baking powder, and salt. Gradually add the dry ingredients to the egg-sugar mixture, stirring after each addition. Scrape the sides of the bowl whenever necessary to make sure the batter is being thoroughly mixed.

Spoon the batter into a 10 by 15 by 1-inch jelly-roll pan, reserving ⅔ cup of the batter. Spread the batter evenly in the pan with a spatula. Then pour the cherry pie filling over the batter, spooning it smoothly all the way to the edges. Then drop teaspoonfuls of the reserved batter over the cherry layer in 4 even rows of 4 dollops each (for a total of 16 spoonfuls on top of the cherry layer). Bake until the edges are slightly brown and begin to pull away from the edge of the pan, about 30 minutes. Remove from oven and let cool.

**To make the glaze:** Melt the butter over low heat in a small saucepan, and then pour into a bowl. Gradually add the powdered sugar, beating well after each addition and scraping down the sides frequently. Add the vanilla. Then add the milk, 1 tablespoon at a time, until the glaze is smooth. Drizzle over the warm coffeecake.

Let the cake cool completely and store in a sealed container or cake safe. This cake will stay fresh for 3 to 4 days.

# Chapter Five

*"We enjoyed the brownies that my daughter Susan made when she came home from school.
It has been a long day for them, so it is an enjoyable snack. By the time they all have a bath, brush their teeth,
and we have our prayers, it is past their bedtime. It's been a long day, but it was enjoyable to work together."*

— LOVINA EICHER, 2007

As the Amish have evolved from an agrarian culture to a more diversified one, culinary habits have changed alongside everything else. Amish men, for instance, used to come in from the fields for a hearty lunch. Often the biggest meal of the day was the noon one (dinner), when hard-working men and teenage boys would refuel for a second shift in the fields. In some settlements now, the men are more likely to be eating their dinner from a lunch bucket in a factory break room than at home. So Amish wives have tried to re-create the noon meal in a lunch bucket for their husbands (see Lunch Buckets, page 165). A hearty lunch-bucket meal might contain a thick sandwich of home-baked bread, cheese, and meat and also a piece of fruit, a drink, and, yes, dessert. Pie is often too messy, cookies too crumbly, and cake requires a fork. So this leaves brownies or bars often as

the sweet treat of choice for the lunch bucket. From moist, chewy chocolate brownies to sweet lemon bars, the bar has evolved into a lunch-bucket favorite.

Bars and brownies have been staples in Amish children's lunch buckets for years for much the same reason. They are a portable sweet treat that can be carried to class and shared for birthdays, Christmas, or other occasions.

The trend toward bars and brownies can also be seen at Amish-owned bakeries.

One Amish-owned bakery in Indiana features "Can't Leave Alone Bars," a gooey confection made of yellow cake mix, sweetened condensed milk, chocolate, vegetable oil, butter, and eggs.

## BARS AND BROWNIES

When I was growing up, it seemed we didn't make many bars or brownies. Cookies were much more popular. But through the years, especially since I've been married, it seems I have made lots of bars and brownies. I think it is because bars and brownies don't take nearly as long to make as cookies. I was never as fond of making cookies because they can take so long to bake a whole batch. It is so much simpler just to do a bar or brownie recipe.

Bars and brownies are sometimes served instead of cookies with our church lunch. There are so many different varieties.

Some favorites in our family are the pecan pie bars, chocolate chip bars, halfway bars, rhubarb squares, and delicious peanut butter swirl bars. My children like almost any bar or brownie. When we try a new recipe, it doesn't take too long for them to disappear in our house. Bars and brownies are always something easy to whip up to take along somewhere. They are also easy to put into lunch buckets or to send as treats at parties in school.

## PECAN PIE BARS
**Makes 20 bars**

*These were always a favorite of mine when they would be served after church. The bars will keep well for several days.*

CRUST:

2 cups all-purpose flour

1 cup packed brown sugar

1 cup butter, softened

FILLING:

5 large eggs

1 cup light corn syrup

1 cup packed brown sugar

¾ cup granulated sugar

Dash of salt

1 teaspoon vanilla extract

1 cup pecan pieces

Preheat the oven to 350°F. Lightly grease a 9 by 13-inch pan and set aside.

**To make the crust:** In a large bowl, combine the flour and brown sugar. Dice the butter into little cubes and cut it into the flour mixture. Using your fingertips, blend until the mixture resembles coarse crumbs. Do not use an electric mixer. Press the flour mixture into the prepared pan and bake for 10 minutes.

**To make the filling:** While the crust is baking, combine the eggs, corn syrup, sugars, salt, and vanilla in a large bowl. Blend well until the mixture is the color of butterscotch. Stir in the pecan pieces. Remove the crust from the oven and pour the filling over the hot crust. Lower the oven temperature to 275°F and bake until the center is set, about 50 minutes. Cool in the pan or on a wire rack before cutting into bars.

Store the bars in a sealed container or cake safe. These will stay fresh for 3 to 4 days.

## BUTTERSCOTCH BROWNIES
### Makes 20 brownies

*Homemade butterscotch has been a favorite among the Amish for as long as I can remember. It's an economical and easy sweet treat to make. It's a good alternative to using chocolate in a dessert.*

4 tablespoons (½ stick) butter

1 cup packed brown sugar

1 large egg, beaten

1 teaspoon vanilla extract

1 cup all-purpose flour

½ teaspoon salt

1 teaspoon baking powder

½ cup walnuts, chopped

Powdered sugar for topping

Preheat the oven to 350°F. Grease a 9 by 13-inch pan and set aside.

In a medium saucepan, melt the butter over medium heat. Add the brown sugar and stir for 1 to 2 minutes, until it has a thick, peanut butter–like consistency. Remove from the heat, and then stir in the beaten egg and vanilla, followed by the flour, salt, and baking powder. Once combined, stir in the nuts. Spread the batter into the prepared pan and bake until the edges begin to brown and a toothpick inserted in the center comes out clean, 25 to 30 minutes. Cut into 2 by 2-inch squares while warm and sprinkle with powdered sugar. Store in an airtight container.

## COOKIE DOUGH BROWNIES

### Makes 2 dozen brownies

*The children like this dessert because, as you can tell by the name, it tastes like cookie dough, but it's a brownie. So it is sort of like having two desserts in one. This is as close to cookie dough as I'll let my children eat. I don't usually let them eat the dough for cookies because it often contains raw eggs.*

| BROWNIES: | FILLING: | GLAZE: |
|---|---|---|
| 2 cups granulated sugar | ½ cup (1 stick) butter, softened | 1 cup chocolate chips |
| ½ cup unsweetened cocoa powder | ½ cup packed brown sugar | 1 tablespoon shortening |
| 1½ cups all-purpose flour | ¼ cup granulated sugar | ¾ cup chopped walnuts (optional) |
| ½ teaspoon salt | 2 tablespoons milk | |
| 1 cup vegetable oil | 1 teaspoon vanilla extract | |
| 4 large eggs | 1 cup all-purpose flour | |
| 2 teaspoons vanilla extract | | |
| ½ cup chopped walnuts (optional) | | |

Preheat the oven to 350°F. Grease a 9 by 13-inch baking pan.

**To make the brownies:** In a bowl, combine the sugar, cocoa, flour, and salt. Add the oil, eggs, and vanilla. Combine the ingredients until well blended. Stir in walnuts if desired. Spread into the prepared pan. Bake until a toothpick inserted in the center comes out clean, about 30 minutes. Let the brownies cool while preparing the filling.

**To make the filling:** Cream the butter and sugars together, and then add the milk and vanilla. Stir in the flour until the filling resembles cookie dough. Spread the filling evenly over the entire pan of cooled brownies. Place in the refrigerator for 15 to 20 minutes or until firm to the touch. While the brownies are refrigerated, prepare the glaze.

**To make the glaze:** In a small saucepan, melt the chocolate chips and shortening over low heat. Quickly spread the glaze over the filling, as the filling will soften from the heat of the glaze. Sprinkle and press the walnuts on top. Place the brownies back in the refrigerator until the glaze has set up.

Store the brownies in a sealed container or cake safe. These will stay fresh for 3 to 4 days.

## HONEY BARS

### Makes 2 dozen bars

*Some Amish do keep bees so that they can make and sell their own honey. Pure homemade honey tastes delicious. I often use honey in place of molasses in recipes because we seem to prefer the taste. This bar is delicious with a strong taste of honey.*

1 cup granulated sugar

2 cups all-purpose flour

1 teaspoon baking soda

1¼ teaspoon ground cinnamon

1 large egg, lightly beaten

¾ cup vegetable oil

¼ cup honey

1 cup walnuts, chopped

GLAZE:

1 cup powdered sugar

1 teaspoon vanilla extract

1 tablespoon water

2 tablespoons mayonnaise

Preheat the oven to 350°F.

In a large bowl, stir the sugar, flour, baking soda, and cinnamon until evenly mixed. Then add in the egg, vegetable oil, honey, and nuts. Stir until the mixture is smooth. Spoon into an ungreased jelly-roll pan or 9 by 13-inch pan. Bake until a toothpick inserted in the center comes out clean, about 20 minutes.

**To make the glaze:** In a small bowl, stir together the powdered sugar, vanilla, water, and mayonnaise until smooth and creamy. Spread onto the honey bars while they are still warm.

Store the bars in a sealed container or cake safe. These will stay fresh for 3 to 4 days.

## BASIC BROWNIES

### Makes 2 dozen brownies

*This is a great recipe to use as the first one to teach children to bake. The ingredients are simple ones and the batter takes just a few minutes to mix. The result is a sweet and chewy chocolate brownie, the type of snack that doesn't last very long around here!*

1½ cups all-purpose flour

2 cups sugar

½ cup unsweetened cocoa powder

½ teaspoon salt

1 cup vegetable oil

4 large eggs

2 teaspoons vanilla extract

½ cup chopped walnuts (optional)

Preheat the oven to 350°F. Grease a 9 by 13-inch pan.

In a large bowl, combine all the ingredients. Stir vigorously for about 3 minutes, until the batter is well blended and creamy. Pour into the prepared pan. Bake until a knife inserted into the center comes out clean, about 30 minutes.

Store the brownies in a sealed container or cake safe. These will stay fresh for 3 to 4 days.

## DELICIOUS PECAN BROWNIES

### Makes 2 dozen brownies

*Never use a glass pan for this recipe, because the brownies just seem to get too hard. But the brownies are delicious and chewy every time when I make these using a stainless steel or aluminum pan.*

BROWNIES:

1 cup (2 sticks) butter, softened

2 cups granulated sugar

4 large eggs

1 cup semisweet chocolate chips, melted

2 teaspoons vanilla extract

1 cup all-purpose flour

1 cup chopped pecans

FROSTING:

3 cups powdered sugar

⅓ cup butter, softened

2 ounces semisweet chocolate chips, melted

3 to 4 tablespoons milk

1 teaspoon vanilla extract

Preheat the oven to 350°F. Grease a 9 by 13-inch pan.

**To make the brownies:** In a large bowl, cream the butter and sugar. Beat in the eggs until the mixture is smooth and creamy. Then blend in the melted chocolate and vanilla. Stir in the flour and nuts. Pour into the prepared pan. Bake for 30 minutes. Remove from the oven and allow the brownies to cool to room temperature.

**To make the frosting:** Mix the powdered sugar, butter, melted chocolate, milk, and vanilla until smooth and creamy. Apply the frosting to the cooled brownies with a butter knife or the back of a spoon.

Store the brownies in a sealed container or cake safe. These will stay fresh for 7 days.

## 10-MINUTE COOKIE BARS

### Makes 2 dozen bars

*This is another good teaching recipe. Children as young as 7 or 8 can easily mix up the batter and frosting for this recipe. It's good to start giving them experience baking at an early age.*

### BROWNIES:

1 cup packed brown sugar

4 cups quick-cooking rolled oats

1 cup (2 sticks) butter, softened

### FROSTING:

1 cup chocolate chips

½ cup creamy peanut butter

Preheat the oven to 400°F.

**To make the brownies:** Combine the brown sugar and oats in a large bowl. Melt the butter in a small saucepan, then pour into a large bowl. Pour over the brown sugar and oats, and mix well. Press the mixture into an ungreased 9 by 13 by 2-inch pan. Bake for 10 minutes.

**To make the frosting:** Melt the chocolate chips and peanut butter together in a saucepan. Spread the frosting over the baked layer and chill.

Store the bars in a sealed container or cake safe. These will stay fresh for 3 to 4 days.

# REGIONAL DIFFERENCES IN AMISH BAKING: INDIANA VS. MICHIGAN

Different Amish communities allow different things. Where we lived in Indiana, the church did not allow gas stoves or indoor plumbing. Here in our community in Michigan, the Amish are allowed these two things.

A gas stove is so much easier to use than a kerosene stove. With the kerosene you had to tilt the glass globe back, light the wick, wait for the flame go all around the wick, and then gradually turn it up. My stove had a 1-gallon kerosene tank, and it never failed that whenever I was in a hurry it would run out. Then we'd have to go outside to the tank, fill it, come back inside, and light the kerosene stove all over again. The kerosene seemed to go out most often when I was getting Joe's breakfast ready and time was limited. After awhile, I started keeping a little jug of kerosene in the garage so that I could at least fill the stove quickly in a pinch. One of my stoves had a glass kerosene holder so that you could at least see when the kerosene was getting low. The other one, unfortunately, was black and you couldn't see the level at all. With a gas stove, our tank still needs to be filled, but it usually doesn't run out in the middle of preparing a meal. Gas ovens, I have found, bake a lot more evenly. With the kerosene ovens, I'd have to turn a cake around halfway through the baking time so that it would bake evenly. With a gas stove, I can just leave it in there and let it bake.

The gas stoves are also safer in a house full of children. If a child turns my stove up high here, it will not start a fire instantly. With the kerosene stoves I can remember a time or two when I turned away for a minute and one of the children turned the knob on the kerosene stove and suddenly the kitchen was full of smoke. I had to keep a constant eye on the children while in the kitchen baking. For instance, I could never have put a cake in the oven in Indiana and gone out of the room until it was done, like I can here.

The kerosene stoves have a hard, clear plastic that was almost like Plexiglas. It would not burn and was on the front part of the burner so the flame could be watched. I tell you, every single time any of my children would start walking or crawling, the first thing they would do is punch out the Plexiglas and then it would have to be replaced.

Not all of the kerosene stove memories, though, are bad ones. My daughter Susan said she still remembers how we always made toast right over the burner and flipped it over using two forks because it would be so hot. Susan also remembers sitting on the floor and looking up and telling me when the toast was brown enough to turn. And I remember doing that same thing when I was a child, sitting on the floor looking up at my mother.

Another good memory of those stoves would be the smell. I would like to come downstairs when Mom was lighting all the burners. I liked the smell of the match; it was a good smell for me. There was only a certain type of match she would buy, but I can't remember what kind.

Having running water inside is something that makes things easier now too. It hasn't changed the way I bake, but I can do a lot more baking at one time because I know I have enough hot water to wash the dishes right away. Without running water I used to have to heat the water and bring it all to the sink to start washing. Having running water just saves a lot of steps. The same is true with having a gas refrigerator and freezer. When we were children, we could never buy ice cream to store because there was no place to keep it. We could only buy what we could eat right away. We only made home-made ice cream during the winter when there was a lot of ice. We kept a block of ice in the basement throughout the year, and that would keep some foods cold. But we'd have to go to the basement for salad dressings, to the milk barn for milk, and to the henhouse for eggs. Now we still have to go the henhouse, but the eggs can be stored in the gas refrigerator inside.

I often think our lifestyle just changes with the times. For instance, back when my grandmother and grandfather were being raised, non-Amish people were being raised in a way similar to them. But as the years pass, the Amish get a little more technology as decided by our church congregation.

## CHOCOLATE CHIP BARS

**Makes 20 bars**

*These are good with or without icing. My daughter Elizabeth likes to make these for her brothers and sisters.*

½ teaspoon salt

½ teaspoon baking soda

1 cup packed brown sugar

1 large egg

½ cup shortening, softened

1 teaspoon vinegar

½ cup sour milk

1 teaspoon vanilla extract

1¾ cups all-purpose flour

1 cup chocolate chips

Preheat the oven to 350°F. Grease a 10 by 15-inch baking sheet.

Mix the salt, baking soda, brown sugar, egg, shortening, vinegar, sour milk, and vanilla in a large bowl. Then stir in the flour, followed by the chocolate chips. Spread the batter evenly into the prepared pan. Bake until the edges are golden brown and the chips are melted, 20 minutes. Let cool, and then cut into bars.

Store the bars in a sealed container or cake safe. These will stay fresh for 3 to 4 days.

## LUNCH BUCKETS

Long before fast-food and chicken by the bucket, there was the lunch bucket. For generations, Amish homemakers have packed lunch pails with a midday meal that's balanced to provide enough sustenance and sweetness to get through the rest of a rigorous workday.

An Amish homemaker in Adams County, Ohio, packs four lunch buckets each day, but she has seen a trend toward healthier snacks to replace the baked goods. "Jell-O with fruit is healthier," says Leah Miller.

Another young Amish homemaker always makes sure she puts a cookie, usually a molasses cookie, in with her husband's lunch. "That's his favorite," she says sheepishly.

Bobby Miller, 20, a young Amish man in Adams County, Ohio, likes to find baked goods in his lunch bucket. Homemade chocolate chip cookies are a favorite.

With the trend toward more factory work in the Amish community, something new has emerged: the breakfast bucket.

Lovina has found herself packing a breakfast bucket for Joe. Here's how she describes it:

"My husband leaves for work so early that he sometimes doesn't get a chance to eat breakfast before work, so I pack him a breakfast and a lunch. So I will send along some hard-boiled eggs or a bacon and cheese sandwich for his breakfast, which he'll eat on his first break. Sometimes I'll send scrambled eggs, also." Lovina adds that she always tries to put fruit and a sweet in the lunch bucket and that Joe's Amish co-workers always bring in new baked-goods desserts to try.

"So he comes home telling me, you'll have to make this dessert that I saw in someone's lunch bucket," she says.

## CHOCOLATE CHIP OATMEAL BROWNIES
### Makes 2 dozen brownies

*This is a favorite of the children's. It makes a great after-school snack with a cold glass of milk! This also a fun recipe to experiment with by using peanut butter or butterscotch chips instead of chocolate chips.*

1 cup (2 sticks) butter, softened

⅔ cup granulated sugar

⅔ cup packed dark brown sugar

2 large eggs

½ teaspoon vanilla extract

1 cup all-purpose flour

1 teaspoon baking powder

¼ teaspoon ground nutmeg

1 teaspoon ground cinnamon

2 cups quick-cooking rolled oats

2 cups semisweet chocolate chips

Preheat the oven to 350°F. Lightly grease a 9 by 13-inch pan and set aside.

In a large bowl, beat the butter, sugars, and eggs until fluffy. Stir in the vanilla. Then blend in the flour, baking powder, nutmeg, cinnamon, and oats with a wooden spoon. Blend in 1 cup of the chocolate chips. The batter will be thick. Electric mixers are not recommended for mixing the batter. Once the mixture is well blended, spread with a spoon into the prepared pan. Sprinkle the top with the remaining 1 cup of the chocolate chips. Bake until a butter knife inserted in the center comes out clean, about 30 minutes.

Store the brownies in a sealed container or cake safe. These will stay fresh for 3 to 4 days.

## RHUBARB SQUARES

**Makes 2 dozen squares**

*Rhubarb finds its way into so many baked goods. It just adds a nice, tart taste to everything. Mom baked with her homegrown rhubarb often, and she never had trouble growing rhubarb. If you want to start your own rhubarb patch, plant the rhubarb one year and then use it the second year. I have always done this and always had good luck. You don't use the rhubarb for a year so that you can give the plants time to develop strong roots. I got my starts from a lady in church and just planted a whole row of them, and every year they get fuller and spread out more. I plant my rhubarb in full sun, because I don't think the plants do as well in the shade. A lot of times people will plant them right at the edge of their garden. We do this and also put horse manure around the plants in the spring, which seems to help them grow. The rhubarb is one of the first goodies ready to be harvested in the spring, and this recipe is a great way to starting using it.*

FILLING:
4 cups rhubarb cut into ¼-inch pieces
2 cups water
1 cup granulated sugar
3 tablespoons cornstarch
½ teaspoon almond extract

CRUST:
¾ cup shortening, softened
1 cup packed brown sugar
1 teaspoon baking soda
1 teaspoon vanilla extract
1 cup all-purpose flour

1 cup quick-cooking rolled oats
1 teaspoon ground cinnamon

Preheat the oven to 350°F. Lightly grease a 9 by 13-inch pan and set aside.

**To make the filling:** In a medium saucepan over low heat, cook the rhubarb, water, and sugar until bubbling. Then add the cornstarch and stir until the cornstarch is mixed throughout and the mixture has thickened. Add the almond flavoring and stir. Keep on the stove over low heat.

**To make the crust:** In a large bowl, combine the shortening, sugar, baking soda, vanilla, flour, oats, and cinnamon until the mixture forms coarse crumbs. Take half of the crumbs and pat them into the bottom of the prepared pan. Remove the filling from the heat and pour over the bottom crust, spreading it evenly. Then crumble the remaining half of the crumbs evenly over the filling. Bake until the crust is golden and a toothpick inserted in the center comes out clean, about 40 minutes.

Store the brownies in a sealed container or cake safe. These will stay fresh for 3 to 4 days.

## HALFWAY BARS
### Makes 2 dozen bars

*I still remember the first time I made these. I was helping out at my brother Amos's house when they were remodeling. There was a crew there working on their house. My sister-in-law had me mix this recipe together, and I really liked them. I asked her if I could have the recipe, and now we really make these a lot. They are halfway between a bar and a cookie, which is how they got their name. They taste a bit like a cookie, but you cut them like bars. I made these several times when we had the crew working on our house too; they were something warm to take out to the guys when they were working. They thought it was a real treat.*

1 cup (2 sticks) butter, softened

½ cup packed brown sugar

½ cup granulated sugar

1 teaspoon vanilla extract

¼ teaspoon salt

¼ teaspoon baking soda

1 teaspoon baking powder

2 egg yolks

1 teaspoon water

2½ cups all-purpose flour

1 cup chocolate chips

GLAZE:

2 egg whites

1 cup brown sugar

Preheat the oven to 350°F. Grease a 9 by 13-inch baking pan.

In a small saucepan, melt the butter. Pour the melted butter into a large bowl. In a small bowl, separate the eggs, reserving the whites for the glaze. Add the sugars, vanilla, salt, baking soda, baking powder, 2 egg yolks, water, and flour to form a stiff dough. Spread the dough into the prepared baking pan. Spread the chocolate chips evenly over the dough.

**To make the glaze:** In a small bowl, beat the 2 egg whites into the brown sugar. Pour the glaze over the bars. Bake until a toothpick inserted in the center comes out clean, about 35 minutes.

Store the bars in a sealed container or cake safe. These will stay fresh for 3 to 4 days.

## LEMON SQUARES

**Makes 16 squares**

*Lemon can make for a nice, light dessert during the summer months. Sometimes after an exhausting day's work outside, a snack sounds good, but not something heavy like pound cake or cookies. These lemon squares with their light, fluffy filling are a great treat!*

CRUST:

1¼ cups powdered sugar

Pinch of salt

½ cup all-purpose flour

½ cup (1 stick) plus 1 tablespoon butter
  or margarine

FILLING:

1 cup granulated sugar

¼ cup fresh lemon juice

½ teaspoon baking powder

2 large eggs, slightly beaten

GLAZE:

¾ cup powdered sugar, sifted

2 tablespoons fresh lemon juice

1 tablespoon butter, melted

Preheat the oven to 350°F. Line an 8-inch square cake pan with parchment paper. Make sure an inch of paper overlaps the edges so that the bars can be lifted out when they are done.

**To make the crust:** In a large bowl, combine the sugar, salt, flour, and butter together until dry, coarse crumbs form. Press firmly into the prepared pan. Bake for 15 minutes. Let cool for a few minutes before adding the filling.

**To make the filling:** Whisk together the sugar, lemon juice, baking powder, and eggs in a bowl until the sugar has completely dissolved. Pour over the crust. Bake until the filling is nearly set but still jiggles a little, 25 to 30 minutes. Let cool completely.

**To make the glaze:** In a small bowl, mix the powdered sugar, lemon juice, and butter until evenly blended. Pour over the cooled filling. Let set until room temperature. Lift from the pan and cut into bars.

Store the squares in a sealed container or cake safe. These will stay fresh for 3 to 4 days.

## OATMEAL BARS

### Makes 2 dozen bars

*I always have quick-cooking oatmeal in my pantry, and it is just so handy for making a quick snack for the children. Oatmeal can be used for cookies, bars, and cakes in a pinch. This is a surprisingly chewy and moist snack.*

1¼ cups boiling water

1 cup quick-cooking rolled oats

½ cup (1 stick) butter, softened

1 cup granulated sugar

1 cup packed brown sugar

2 large eggs

1½ cups all-purpose flour

1 teaspoon baking soda

½ teaspoon salt

1 teaspoon vanilla extract

ICING:

6 tablespoons butter

1 cup packed brown sugar

¼ cup milk or cream

1 cup powdered sugar

Preheat the oven to 350°F.

In a medium bowl, pour the boiling water over the oats and butter. Let set until room temperature. In a large bowl, cream together the sugars, eggs, flour, baking soda, salt, and vanilla. Add the oat mixture and stir to blend. Pour the mixture onto a 10 by 15-inch baking sheet. Bake until brown, 20 to 30 minutes. Let cool before frosting.

**To make the icing:** In a small saucepan, bring the butter, brown sugar, and milk to a boil over low heat. Let boil for 2 minutes, and then remove from the heat. Add the powdered sugar and stir to blend and dissolve. Spread the icing over the cooled bars.

Store the bars in a sealed container or cake safe. These will stay fresh for 3 to 4 days.

### CHILDREN'S BAKING
### Joseph, 6

*I want to learn how to make cookies and pies. I don't know how but it looks fun. I stirred my birthday cake when I turned six.*

## FRUIT-FILLED OATMEAL SQUARES

### Makes 2 dozen squares

*I like to use homemade pie filling for this recipe, but you can use store-bought too. You can experiment with this recipe using whatever fruit filling you choose.*

½ cup (1 stick) butter, softened
¼ cup all-purpose flour
1 cup packed brown sugar
1½ cups quick-cooking rolled oats
1 (21-ounce) can apple pie filling

Preheat the oven to 325°F.

In a large bowl, combine the butter, flour, brown sugar, and oats until mixed evenly and the texture resembles coarse crumbs. Press two-thirds of the mixture into an ungreased 9-inch square pan. Pour the pie filling over the crumbs in the pan. Then sprinkle the remaining crumbs on top. Bake until the oatmeal topping begins to turn golden brown, about 25 minutes. Cool completely and cut into squares.

Store the squares in a sealed container or cake safe. These will stay fresh for 3 to 4 days.

## TOFFEE NUT BARS
### Makes 2 dozen bars

*This is a favorite dessert because it's a sweet treat that is a change from chocolate. Before chocolate became popular among the Amish, desserts like this one (and also desserts with molasses) were more common.*

**CRUST:**

½ cup (1 stick) butter, softened

½ cup packed brown sugar

1 cup all-purpose flour

**TOPPING:**

2 large eggs

1 cup packed brown sugar

1 teaspoon vanilla extract

2 tablespoons all-purpose flour

1 teaspoon baking powder

½ teaspoon salt

1 cup shredded coconut,
    unsweetened

1 cup almonds, slivered

Preheat the oven to 350°F.

**To make the crust:** In a small bowl, stir together the butter, brown sugar, and flour until the ingredients are evenly mixed. Press and flatten by hand into the bottom of an ungreased 9 by 13-inch pan. Bake for 10 to 12 minutes, checking for firmness at 10 minutes.

**While the crust is baking, make the topping:** In a large bowl, beat the eggs and then stir in the brown sugar, vanilla, flour, baking powder, salt, coconut, and almonds. Remove the crust from the oven and spread the topping evenly over the crust. Be careful not to tear the crust. Return to the oven and bake until the topping is golden brown, 23 to 25 minutes. Watch carefully, as the top will easily burn. Cut while warm and store in an airtight container.

Store the bars in a sealed container or cake safe. These will stay fresh for 3 to 4 days.

## DELICIOUS PEANUT BUTTER SWIRL BARS

### Makes 2 dozen bars

*These bars are very pretty with their dark chocolate swirls throughout. The dessert is a sweet treat to add to any lunch-bucket meal!*

1 cup creamy peanut butter

⅔ cup butter, softened

1½ cups packed brown sugar

1½ cups granulated sugar

4 large eggs

4 teaspoons vanilla extract

2 cups all-purpose flour

2 teaspoons baking powder

½ teaspoon salt

1 (12-ounce) package semisweet chocolate chips

Preheat the oven to 325°F. Grease a 9 by 13-inch pan and set aside.

In a large bowl, cream together the peanut butter, butter, and sugars until well blended and smooth. Make sure any lumps of brown sugar are dissolved. Then add the eggs and vanilla. Mix until smooth and creamy and thoroughly blended. Add the flour, baking powder, and salt. Mix thoroughly until the batter is once again smooth and creamy. Spoon the batter into the prepared pan. Sprinkle the chocolate chips over the batter and put into the oven for 5 minutes.

Remove from the oven and, using a butter knife, swirl the chocolate chips through the dough. Return to the oven and bake until a butter knife inserted into the center comes out clean (some chocolate may stick to the knife), about 40 minutes. Let cool for 1 hour and cut into bars.

Store the bars in a sealed container or cake safe. These will stay fresh for 3 to 4 days.

## BUTTERMILK BROWNIES

**Makes 2 dozen brownies**

*This recipe provides another way to use leftover buttermilk. Buttermilk always makes baked goods taste very moist. This is more like a cake than a brownie.*

2 cups sugar

2 cups all-purpose flour

¼ cup unsweetened cocoa powder

1 cup cold water

½ cup (1 stick) butter, softened

½ cup vegetable oil

½ cup buttermilk

1 teaspoon baking soda

2 large eggs

1 teaspoon vanilla extract

Dash of salt

Preheat the oven to 400°F. Lightly grease a 9 by 13-inch pan.

In a large bowl, sift together the sugar, flour, and cocoa. In a small saucepan, bring the water, butter, and oil to a boil over low heat. Remove from the heat after the mixture has boiled for 1 full minute. Pour the hot mixture over the dry ingredients and beat until smooth and creamy. Add the buttermilk, baking soda, eggs, vanilla, and salt. Stir thoroughly. Spoon the mixture into the prepared pan and bake until a butter knife inserted in the center comes out clean, about 20 minutes.

Store the brownies in a sealed container or cake safe. These will stay fresh for 3 to 4 days.

## CHILDREN'S BAKING
### Elizabeth, 14

*I have learned many lessons in my few years of baking. The older I get, the more I am trying a new variety of things to bake. One thing I have learned is that you have to pay very close attention to what a recipe says. Sometimes one thing can be wrong and your whole batter goes to waste. However, sometimes batter with incorrect ingredients can still be used by adding something else to it.*

*When I was a little girl, probably around the age of four or five, I would push a footstool up to the counter so I could stand and watch Mom roll cookie dough into small round balls. It always looked very fun to me. Now I have mostly taken over the job of baking cookies around this house. I still sometimes will ask Mom a question if I am not too familiar with a recipe. Mother taught me to always bake only one first as a test it to see if it is right. If the one cookie doesn't turn out, then often it is not too late to adjust the ingredients. I have found out that if you are baking cookies and they keep going flat, it is time to add more flour or oatmeal. Also it can be something as simple as needing to bake the cookie a little longer. Sometimes if the dough is too sticky you have to chill it for a while and then the dough will be easier to handle.*

*Another lesson I learned early on is that when a recipe calls for egg yolks it means only the yolks and not the whites. The whites can be saved for other recipes. When I first started baking, I kept mixing up the abbreviations for tablespoons and teaspoons, which made some* baking tricky. So luckily I asked Mom before I put a tablespoon of something into the batter that was actually supposed to be a teaspoon. One time when I was mixing a bread recipe I put in 2 tablespoons of salt and 1 teaspoon of sugar, but it turned out the recipe actually called for the reverse. Later on Mom wondered why the bread was not rising too much. Then I looked the recipe over and saw what I had done!

The next thing I would like to start learning is how to make pie dough. I help Mom put the dough into the pie pans after it is rolled out. And I crimped the pie dough for the first time not too long ago. I used to think it looked so fun when Mom did it. It was kind of fun and easier than I thought it would be. I have many years of baking ahead of me, but I am thankful for the many lessons I have already learned to make me a better baker.

## SPECIAL OCCASIONS

# Chapter Six

*"On my agenda this week is to start cutting out my navy blue dress, cape, and apron for niece Elizabeth's wedding next week. I have to help cook at the wedding and we are to wear dark blue dresses. Since mine isn't in very good shape any more for a wedding, I need to sew me a new one. I hope they will have a nice warm day for their wedding. On October 17, 51 years ago, my parents were united in marriage. They were married 42 years together before Dad's death in 2000. That many years ago there weren't nearly as many guests for their wedding. With so many relatives and friends, weddings can get very large amongst the Amish."*

— LOVINA EICHER, 2008

It has been an honor and a blessing to have come to know Lovina's family through the years. "The Amish Cook" column has not always been easy, but every time I've contemplated perhaps doing something else with my life, I'm always pulled back by the wonderful friendship with the Eichers and their extended family. We've shared some of our most difficult and most celebratory times together. "Special occasions" are not always good, just different. This chapter, however, will celebrate some of the more enjoyable special moments in Amish life while also looking at how food can comfort during sad times.

Weddings are probably the most celebratory events on the Amish calendar. A massive amount of food and labor goes into such an occasion. I will always have very fond memories of attending Lovina and Joe's wedding in July 1993. The experience was a touching tribute to how Amish simplicity and sensibility can infuse an event that is sometimes overly commercialized among the non-Amish with something wonderful and memorable. Among the Amish there are no "bridal expos," $100-a-plate dinners, massive floral arrangements, ice sculptures, or ten-tiered cakes. Yet the Amish version of the event still manages to convey a sense of something very special and poignant as the young couple moves into the next chapter of their lives.

I've learned through the years that the Amish also do other special events in ways that I feel many of us would probably do well to emulate. When a church member is in trouble, help is always close at hand in the form of a frolic, a benefit baking, or prayers. This chapter will explore some of the more moving moments on the Amish calendar.

## CHANGING DESSERTS

Special-occasion desserts have become more expensive and more rich-tasting than they used to be, it seems. I remember attending a wedding where a woman was fixing a very rich dessert, with cake on the bottom, a pudding mixture on top, and another cake layer on top of that, and it was just huge. When I was younger you just didn't see that type of dessert. Now you see all kinds of new recipes being made. It used to be just fruit, pie, and cake for dessert. Mom always said that when she was growing up, they didn't have much dessert. Grandma still taught her how to make desserts, but it was mainly for company. The only time we have dessert, except on rare occasions, is when company comes. Cookies are usually just for a between-meal snack. I don't put desserts on the table after supper very often.

When we did make desserts when I was a child, I remember Mom sifting the flour after she would buy it. They usually just sold unsifted flour back then. Even when I was starting to learn how to bake, we would sometimes have to sift the flour. I always liked to turn the knob of the sifter and make it go around.

This chapter will share a few of the favorite recipes that we usually save for special occasions like church, benefits, quilting bees, or butchering days.

## PREPARING FOR CHURCH

Church services require much work and preparation. Every married couple in the district has to take a turn to hold church. Services are held every other Sunday, so usually we'll have to take a turn twice a year. In some smaller church districts, a person might have to hold services more often. Following is an excerpt from one of Lovina's columns that describes the work and preparation that go into holding a church service.

"Church services were held here yesterday, which is always an event that requires a lot of preparation work.

We set up the church benches in our basement for the services. The benches, dishes for meals, and other supplies needed to hold a service are stored in a wagon that goes from place to place—wherever the services are going to be held. Services are usually around three hours long. Afterward, the menfolk set up four tables, with every table seating sixteen people.

Then the women all pitch in and help get the tables set. It is nice to have most of those dishes we need for lunch stored in containers in the bench wagon. Our menu was coffee, tea, homemade wheat and white bread, bologna, cheese spread, peanut butter spread, dill and sweet pickles, red beets, sweet and hot peppers, butter, homemade jam and sugar, and pumpkin and butterscotch chip cookies.

I also fixed a pot of chicken noodle soup for the younger ones who can't eat sandwiches yet. All in all we had 150 to 175 people show up for services, which is a little lower than usual because some people were gone because of sickness.

After the meal, the men visited with one another while the women helped wash the dishes. Then we served popcorn for a snack. Mid-afternoon everyone went home for a while, but I invited everyone back for supper at 6 P.M. We had pizza casserole, tossed salad, homemade bread, pickles, and dressing. For dessert, chocolate pudding, white and chocolate cake, and ice cream were on the menu. We had plenty of food left.

Quite a few of the families accepted the invitation to come back for supper. We also had the supper in the basement. It sure helps keep the living quarters cleaner when all the church functions can be held in the basement. After supper, the men played games while we women washed dishes. The children played simple games like hide and seek.

We were glad for the cold, 30-degree weather even though Joe had to shovel snow. The freezing weather kept the muddiness in the yard down. Our neighbor came and cleaned our drive of snow the day before. He also made a path to the basement door where everyone came in to put their coats and boots and attend services. Now today we want to mop the floors and do the laundry and get back to normal around here.

After Joe gets home from work, he'll stack all the benches back in the bench wagon. I need to clean the tablecloths and roll them up so they will be ready to use in two weeks at the next place. Dishes also all have to be packed back in the wagon. It's always a relief once everything is back in place, but I enjoy taking our turn to hold church. I appreciate the bread, cookies, and cakes from the church ladies and my sisters. It takes a lot of the load off me.

My neighbor-lady offered to make the cheese spread for me, which took another job off my list. And my family here in Michigan helped with the cleaning before church. With everyone pitching in and helping, it made it a lot easier. Now we want to try to return the favor to others in our church when they need us."

## LONG JOHN ROLLS
### Makes thirty-two 7-inch rolls

*Long John Rolls are often passed around as a snack during quilting bees, sometime before lunch. Sometimes just regular doughnuts would be passed, but I like the Long John Rolls best. I had an aunt who would fill them with cream, and I liked those even better. I would like to try filling mine with cream. Long John Rolls are best when they are fresh, as they dry out fast. They need to be eaten within a day or two of baking. I really do enjoy quilting bees. I think it would be fun to have a lot of ladies over to quilt and to make quilts for my children.*

1 cup lukewarm water

2 packages active dry yeast

1 cup milk

2 large eggs, beaten

½ cup margarine

⅔ cup sugar

½ teaspoon salt

Pinch of ground nutmeg

6 to 7 cups bread flour

Frosting (optional; page 119)

Pour the water into a small bowl, and then add the yeast and stir until completely dissolved. Set aside. Scald the milk and let cool to lukewarm. Add the milk to the dissolved yeast.

Blend together the eggs, margarine, sugar, salt, and nutmeg until well blended, and then add to the milk and yeast mixture. Gradually add the flour until the dough is elastic and easy to handle. Put in a warm place. Cover with wax paper and let rise until double in size, about 2 hours.

Punch down and divide the dough into 2 large pieces. Roll out each piece to a ¾-inch thickness and cut into 7-inch-long oblong pieces. Let rise again.

Heat vegetable shortening in a deep pan to a depth of 2 to 3 inches until very hot. Fry the rolls in batches until golden, 2 minutes on each side. Frosting may be added if desired, once the rolls have cooled.

Long John Rolls cannot be frozen or stored; they should be eaten the day they are made.

## AMISH FUNERAL COOKIES
**Makes 3 dozen**

*Funerals are sad times for family, but they are also a time when everyone pulls together. A service is held usually at the home of the deceased, followed by a large meal for all in attendance. These cookies, which don't need to be baked, are called "funeral cookies" by some because they are able to be made in a hurry to take to a grieving family. Be sure to use quick-cooking oats for this recipe and not instant. The cookies will hold together better.*

½ cup (1 stick) butter

½ cup milk

2 cups sugar

3 tablespoons unsweetened cocoa powder

½ cup creamy peanut butter

1 teaspoon vanilla extract

¼ teaspoon salt

3 cups quick-cooking rolled oats

½ cup chopped pecans

In a small saucepan over medium heat, bring to a boil the butter, milk, sugar, and cocoa, and cook for 1 minute. Remove from the heat and stir in the peanut butter, vanilla, and salt. Mix in the oats and pecans. Drop by the teaspoon onto wax paper and allow the cookies to stand unrefrigerated for 1 hour. After the cookies are set, store in an airtight container with wax paper between the layers.

These cookies will keep for up to 1 week.

## BUTCHERING DAY BAKING

The arrival of "butchering day," usually in January or February, always generated excitement when I was growing up. We would get up really early, around 3 A.M., to prepare for the day.

Dad and my brothers would get the outbuilding ready for the butchering. The scalding tank has to be filled so that the temperature is just right. A lot of people just skin their hogs immediately, but scalding the hogs makes more lard. While the men are scalding, the women and girls are in the house mixing up lard cakes. Mom made these to serve to the men at break time with coffee. She had to time everything just right. Mom had to make sure they were ready right at break time. We girls had the job of rolling them in sugar. Somehow Mom discovered in later years that frying refrigerated tube biscuits and then rolling them in sugar made a really nice substitute for a lard cake.

Lard cakes need to be eaten right away. The leftovers will turn soggy by the next day. Usually Mom would just let them sit out and they would get eaten by the end of the day. I'm not sure why, but lard cakes just became a butchering day tradition. When we went to my aunts' and uncles' houses we would eat lard cakes on butchering day too. The women would bring in the utensils and be cleaning those, and then they would have to stop for the lard-cake break. All of us children looked forward to this day. I remember one year I faked being sick so Mom would keep me home from school because I didn't want to miss out on butchering day.

Mom would cut the lard cakes into any size or shape, and none of them looked alike. Some of them would be a triangle shape, others would be square. She'd always make a slash in the dough before deep-frying it, which helps it to cook through completely. To balance out the sweet taste of the lard cakes, we'd always fry up fresh tenderloin for lunch.

## LARD CAKES
### Makes 2 dozen lard cakes

*Lard cakes actually don't contain any lard: They are just called that because they are traditionally deep-fried in melted lard. You can use vegetable shortening, though, too, but I don't think "vegetable shortening cakes" sounds any better than "lard cakes."*

*Joe and I would like to get a few little pigs to raise for butchering. We usually like to have two a year to butcher. Our first year of marriage, when we did butchering, we had everybody over to help. We would go back and forth with my family, because everyone helps one another with the day of butchering. It would be so much easier to have someone butcher for you. But Joe says he would like to teach his children the steps of going through it. I appreciate what Dad and Mom taught us, so I think maybe the children would be appreciative someday of learning it. And maybe they can keep the tradition of eating lard cakes on butchering day going.*

| | |
|---|---|
| 1½ cups heavy cream | 3 to 4 cups all-purpose flour |
| 2¼ cups sour milk | ½ teaspoon salt |
| 2 heaping teaspoons baking soda | 3 teaspoons sugar, plus sugar for rolling |
| 3 large eggs | Lard or vegetable shortening for frying |

In a large bowl, combine the cream, sour milk, baking soda, eggs, and flour. The consistency should be similar to that of a pie dough, so add a little more flour if needed. Add the salt and sugar. Roll out to a ¼-inch thickness and cut up in any shapes as big as you wish, or into 2 by 4-inch pieces. Cut a 2½-inch slit in the center of each cake. Make sure the slit goes completely through the cake.

Heat the lard in a deep kettle or pan to a depth of about 2 inches until very hot. Fry the cakes in batches until golden, about 1 minute on each side. Roll the cakes in a pan of sugar while still warm. Eat fresh and warm, because they get stale quickly.

## BAKING FOR BENEFIT

Our church holds "baking benefits" for families that need help with hospital bills. An open-heart surgery or cancer treatment can cost a lot, but everyone pitches in to help a needy family with the bills. The benefit is held at the home of a church member. Fry pies (some call them "fried pies") are a popular baked item to offer in exchange for a donation. At one benefit, four or five thousand fry pies were made and distributed. Even some Amish garage sales will have fry pies on hand, with a sign saying that a donation in exchange for a fry pie would be appreciated. I have seen fry pies in many different flavors, among them cherry, blueberry, strawberry, raspberry, and peach. A fry pie is shaped like a half-moon. I had not seen fry pies made when we lived in Indiana, but they seem quite popular among the Amish in Michigan.

A lot of preparation goes into a baking benefit. Announcements are made at churches weeks ahead of time that a "fry pie drive" will be occurring. The day before, there is a lot of preparation with getting everything organized. The women try to start really early in the morning of the benefit day so that the same day the fry pies are made, they can be delivered. At a baking benefit, the ladies, in assembly-line fashion, roll out the dough, put the filling in, crimp the edges, and then deep-fry them. A lot of drivers are lined up who can take the people from house to house to drop off pies. The women plan ahead as to who will take what church district. There are several people who work in teams to deliver to the whole community and then the surrounding churches. They just go up to each house and ask if they want any fry pies. They carry an ice cream bucket with a slash through the lid, and people just put their donations into that. Benefit drives are listed in the local church bulletin, so you want to keep an eye out to see when one is coming up so that you'll know when to expect someone knocking at the door!

## FRY PIES

### Makes 36 pies

*This is the recipe that is most commonly used for a benefit. The pies can be made in almost any assortment of fruit flavor!*

5 cups all-purpose flour

1 teaspoon baking powder

1 teaspoon salt

1 teaspoon sugar

1 cup shortening, softened

2 large eggs, slightly beaten

1 (13-ounce) can evaporated milk

2½ cups fruit filling of your choice (page 27, or use store-bought)

Shortening for frying

In a large bowl, combine the flour, baking powder, salt, and sugar. Cut the shortening into the dry ingredients. In a separate bowl, mix the eggs and evaporated milk together, and then add to the shortening-flour mixture. Mix with a fork just until it holds together and no more. Roll out rather thin, to about a ⅛-inch thickness. Cut out rounds using a 7-inch saucer or circle as a pattern, rerolling the dough as needed. Put ½ cup fruit pie filling on one half of the circle, leaving a bit of space clear around the edge. Be sure your filling is fairly thick and cold or it will run. Fold over the circle and seal the edges well.

Heat shortening in a deep pan to a depth of about 2 inches until very hot. Deep-fry the pies until golden brown on both sides, 2 minutes per side. Put onto a baking sheet or cooling rack to cool before serving.

## WEDDINGS

Weddings are such a blessed, celebratory time in the Amish church, and baked goods are an important part of the day. Probably the most remembered item from weddings when I was growing up are the "nothings." I remember when I was in third grade my sister Leah was married, and that was when I saw them made for the first time in my family. I liked to watch the cooks put the nothings into the deep fryer.

Nothings are stacked six or eight high on plates across the tables. This isn't a dessert that really gets passed around. People throughout the day will just break off a piece. Each nothing is about the size of a dinner plate, so most people just want a piece. Some people compare these to the elephant ears sold at county fairs.

The nothings were made a day or two ahead, when the pies and breads are being baked. I didn't often see them being made as a child because the cooks try to have as few children there as possible because they are busy getting ready for a wedding.

I'll tell a little about the weddings here for those who aren't familiar. Weddings are usually held on Thursdays; this is just a longtime tradition. Everyone is expected to pitch in, including the bride. For instance, at our wedding, before I got dressed I went out with Mom and my sisters in the washhouse and helped get the first skillets of chicken frying. We had 300 pounds of chicken fried for our wedding. The frying began around 4:15 A.M. Mom was probably dressed already in her wedding clothes. By 7 A.M. the bride, groom, and attendants need to be seated because everyone wants to shake hands with the wedding party before sitting down. The bride, groom, and attendants sit for about two hours before the ceremony starts. It was exciting, but I was really nervous.

Joe and I were married closer to noon. In our Michigan Amish community the ceremony ends closer to 11:30 or 11:45, so it is a little shorter. And here in Michigan the bride can choose her wedding dress colors, like hunter green, burgundy, and dark blue. In Indiana, I had to wear black. Here, the bride gets married in a black *kapp*. (Editor's Note: *Kapp* is the German word most Amish use to refer to their head-covering.) After she is married she changes to a white covering and doesn't wear the black one after that. The unmarried women wear black coverings and the married women wear white to church. My daughters wear only black when they go to church and white otherwise. Joe wore a black suit and white shirt on our wedding day.

If you are a designated cook, you don't go in for the service. However, cooks closely related to the bride or groom will go in to see the union of marriage. Here in Michigan the mothers of the bride and groom don't have anything to do, which is actually kind of nice because it gives the parents more time to enjoy the ceremony. My mom never got too much enjoyment out of our weddings because she had to spend the day taking care of everything. Around here each wedding event has a "head cook" to tell everybody what to do. The head cook is usually a close family friend of the bride's. Since the parents don't have a job, they can then sit in the service all day and have time to meet with guests. When my daughters get married, I won't have to do anything, which will be different for me than it was for my mom.

Joe and I had around fourteen couples as table waiters, an unmarried girl and boy who worked together serving the guests, and two water boys who kept water carried to the tables. It's an honor to be chosen as a table waiter, water boy, or cook. We had about thirty cooks at our wedding. To select the cooks you take all your aunts, married sisters, and husband's married sisters and aunts. My mother also chose several ladies who were close friends of hers to be cooks.

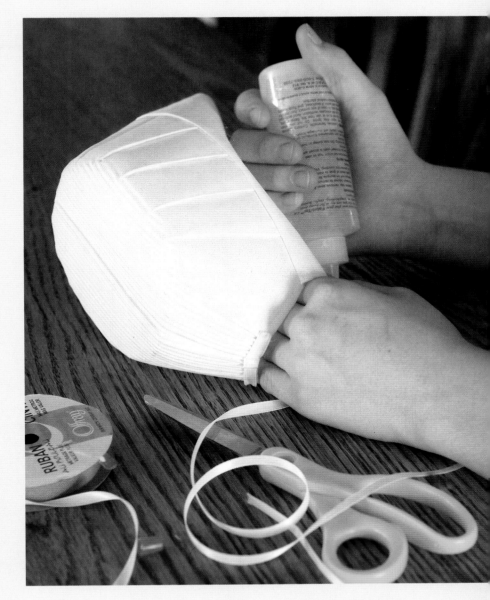

At our wedding there was a large noon meal served, plus a supper for those still in attendance. The noon meal was the largest meal. The menu for both was almost the same, except that ham was a main dish for the evening meal.

We also had so many different kinds of cakes, whatever Mom told them to bring. Weddings also mean baking a lot of cookies, because halfway through the service they'll take a snack out for the younger children and lemonade and coffee for the cooks. Hundreds of cookies have to be made ahead of time and brought in by family members.

Our wedding cake was four layers high. Mom decorated my wedding cake, and I had my side cakes done by a friend. We weren't allowed to have a tiered cake in the church district where we got married; all the cakes had to be the same size, and all white icing. For the side cakes, both had white icing but one was white inside

and one was chocolate. I didn't even cut the side cakes that day. We cut the wedding cake, but the side cakes are for the day after, when both families are there cleaning. Some might freeze them for a while and enjoy them later.

Mom and Dad furnished everything. Sometimes the groom's parents will furnish something like meat, cheese, or potatoes. It really helps when the other family pitches in. To feed all the people who come to a wedding, Mom had stacks and stacks of bowls. If she went to a garage sale, she'd pick up some. You have to borrow kerosene stoves from others for a wedding. Everyone in the area who had an extra kerosene stove chipped in We needed at least ten kerosene stoves. But you want ovens also, portable ovens.

In the community I grew up in, after all the guests were fed in the evening, the table waiters and young folks would all sit around a table and sing songs. While they were singing, the bride and

## NOON DINNER MENU

| | | |
|---|---|---|
| 300 pounds of fried chicken | Green beans | Tapioca pudding |
| Mashed potatoes | Swiss and hot pepper cheeses | Variety of cakes |
| Chicken and noodles | Lettuce salad | Fruit salad |
| Gravy | Carrot salad | Nothings |
| Dressing | Potato salad | Raisin, rhubarb, oatmeal, and cherry pies— |
| Corn | Celery sticks | ninety pies for both meals |
| | Bread and butter and rhubarb jam | |

groom would cut their wedding cake and the pieces would all be laid out on a big tray and passed around. The bride would slip a ring into a piece of the cake before passing out the cake to the young folks. The girl or boy who got the ring in the piece of cake was teased about being the next one to get married. This is all in fun and a tradition passed down in that community. This ring is the only piece of jewelry an Amish bride will ever buy. The ring is a very cheap one and is not worn by the receiver, but is only stored away among other memories.

## NOTHINGS

### Makes 6 or 7 pastries

*This is the recipe for the special, deep-fried wedding pastry. In some areas they are known as "knee patches." We usually just call them by their Swiss name, which is knie platz, which is probably where the English name "knee patches" came from.*

1 large egg
3 cook's spoons (large kitchen spoons) cream
Pinch of salt
Enough all-purpose flour to make a stiff dough
Shortening, for frying
Sugar, for sprinkling

Beat the egg, and then stir in the cream and salt. Add enough flour to the mixture to make a stiff dough. Work it well with your hands. Divide the dough into 6 or 7 balls, and roll out each ball until very thin. Cut 3 slits into each flat piece of dough.

Heat shortening in a deep pan to a depth of 6 inches until very hot. Drop the pieces of dough in, one at a time. Cook until golden on both sides, about 1 full minute on each side minutes. Sprinkle with sugar and stack on a plate.

## OATMEAL PIE

**Makes one 9-inch pie**

*This pie was served at our wedding. It's an old favorite that some people say tastes a lot like pecan pie. It's a very sweet, rich pie. Oatmeal pie was also the first recipe that Mom had in her column when it began back in 1991. This is that same recipe.*

1 disk My Homemade Pie Dough (page 3) or Pat-a-Pan Piecrust (page 4)

2 large eggs

¾ cup dark brown sugar

½ cup (1 stick) butter, softened

¾ cup dark corn syrup

1 cup quick-cooking rolled oats

Preheat the oven to 325°F.

**For the homemade pie dough crust:** Roll the disk of pie dough out to a ⅛-inch thickness on a floured surface. Fit the dough into a 9-inch pie pan. Trim the overhang to 1 inch. Fold the dough under and crimp the edges.

**For the pat-a-pan piecrust:** Pat the dough with your fingers, first at the sides of the 9-inch pie pan and then across the bottom. Flute the edges.

In a large bowl, cream together the eggs, sugar, and butter. Add the corn syrup and oats and mix well until the mixture is well blended and brown in color. Pour into the unbaked pie shell. Bake until a toothpick inserted in the center comes out clean, about 1 hour.

This pie can be stored in a sealed container or cake safe and will stay fresh for up to 10 days.

## VISIT TO A WEDDING WAGON

Jo Ann Yoder is a busy woman from April through October, the traditional season for weddings in the Amish community. June is traditionally the peak month, but with many Amish weddings being held at least partially outdoors, Yoder's services are in high demand anytime the weather is nice. Yoder owns a "cook wagon" or "wedding wagon," which is rented out to blissful brides and grooms for their special day. The wagon—which is transported to sites by a non-Amish hauler—comes complete with everything that is needed for the occasion. There are five gas stoves, plenty of cookware (spoons, knives, cutting boards), and one ginormous coffeemaker.

"People can't get over how quickly that can get a warm cup of coffee brewed," Yoder says, but it's not just one cup; the top-flight coffeemaker is large enough to brew 160 cups of coffee at once.

Another feature of the wedding wagon is plenty of workspace. Yoder says that peeling potatoes is one of the biggest jobs at any Amish wedding. Hundreds of potatoes need to be peeled.

The wagon has two lattice-door entrances so that cooks and come and go during the busy day. "This wagon can easily accommodate a wedding for seven hundred guests," Yoder says. Wedding wagons are rented for a week at a time, so cooks have plenty of time for pre-wedding preparations.

"We've heard a lot about weddings," Yoder says, with a laugh. "We'll be prepared for our own children's someday, definitely."

## HOMEMADE WEDDING ROLLS
### Makes 24 rolls

*Most of the food for weddings here in Michigan is prepared in the "wedding wagons," but one item is baked in the home: the wedding rolls. In the kitchen, the tables are covered with the laid-out, rising roll dough. The women bake them and take them out of the oven. At least a few hundred have to be made for each wedding. The dinner rolls are then served nice and fresh in baskets all around the tables with butter in the baskets. After one wedding meal was over, all of us cooks were allowed to take a basket off a table as a keepsake. As far as dinner rolls go, this really is an easy one to make, but it's such a special treat.*

2 cups warm water
2 packages active dry yeast
½ cup sugar
3 teaspoons salt
¼ cup vegetable oil
1 large egg
6½ to 7 cups bread flour

In a large bowl, combine the water, yeast, sugar, salt, oil, and egg until the mixture is well blended. Add 3 to 4 cups of flour and mix well. Then add the remaining flour and mix until an elastic dough forms. Cover the bowl and let the dough rise for about 2 hours.

Preheat the oven to 400°F. Shape the dough into fist-size rolls. Let them rise again until double in size, about 1 hour. Bake until golden, 13 to 15 minutes.

# THE AMISH COOK'S BAKING TIPS AND TABLE

I try to make sure I have all of the ingredients I need before I start baking. But sometimes I realize that I don't have one or two of the ingredients I need. There are some easy substitutions that can be made for certain items. For instance, if a recipe calls for molasses and I don't have any, I almost always use honey in its place. In recipes that call for squares of baking chocolate, I just use the same amount of chocolate chips in its place and the recipe turns out just fine. Here are some other suggestions:

**Baking Powder (1 teaspoon):** Use ⅓ teaspoon baking soda and ½ teaspoon cream of tartar.

**Brown Sugar (1 cup):** Use 1 cup granulated sugar and 2 tablespoons dark corn syrup or molasses.

**Buttermilk (1 cup):** Use 1 cup thick sour milk.

**Cake Flour (1 cup):** Put 2 tablespoons cornstarch in a cup and fill with all-purpose flour.

**Chocolate (1 ounce):** For a semisweet square, use 3 tablespoons cocoa powder and 1 tablespoon butter, or ½ cup chocolate chips.

**Corn Syrup (1 cup):** Use 1 cup of honey or molasses.

**Cream (1 cup):** Use ¾ cup milk and 4 tablespoons softened butter; or melt the butter and add it to the milk.

**Honey (1 cup):** Use 1 cup light corn syrup or molasses.

**Lemon (1 teaspoon juice):** Use 1 teaspoon grated lemon peel or ½ teaspoon lemon extract.

**Milk (1 cup whole milk):** Use ¾ cup water and 2 tablespoons melted shortening.

**Powdered Sugar:** Combine 1 cup sugar and 1 tablespoon cornstarch and blend together until powdery, makes 1⅓ cups of powdered sugar.

**Self-rising Flour (1 cup):** Use 1 cup all-purpose flour with 1½ teaspoons baking powder and salt added.

**Shortening (1 cup):** Use 1 cup margarine, ¾ cup chicken lard, 1 cup softened butter, or 1 cup vegetable oil.

**Sour Milk (1 cup):** Use 1 cup plain yogurt, or add 1 tablespoon vinegar to 1 cup milk and let stand for 15 minutes.

**Sugar (1 cup):** Use 1 cup honey or corn syrup.

**Vinegar (1 tablespoon):** Use 1 tablespoon fresh lemon juice.

# Index